Up Through The Cracks

Up Through The Cracks

Jack Reynolds

To order additional copies of this book, contact:
Xlibris Corporation
1-888-795-4274
www.Xlibris.com
Orders@Xlibris.com
39370

Short Story Index

6/11/90-07

~~~~~~~~~~IN MEMORY OF~~~~~~~~~~
MY MOTHER…MY FATHER…MY BROTHER…MY DAUGHTER…MY
FRIENDS

RUTH REYNOLDS
CHARLES REYNOLDS
LARRY REYNOLDS
SHERRY REYNOLDS
EDDIE BROOKS
RONALD ALLEN (EL-TEZ)

~~~~~~~~~~DEDICATED TO~~~~~~~~~~
THE FAMILY

The civil rights movement had turned into a mirage. As soon as the seats of success became available, blacks took their places among those we were fighting. It's easy to look down at those who have very little. Self-recognition causes fools to stick out their chest and boost. "I'm better than they are. I'm smarter than they are. I've been given a good well paying job because I'm different than most of them. I don't talk like them, dress like them, act like them, I don't like their music . . . and . . . I hate niggas too. They're lazy and don't want anything. They're uneducated and live on welfare and they commit nearly all the crimes, we all know this. They should put them away forever. More prisons, we need curfews, more cops. They're drug users, suppliers and growers and . . . my how they love alcohol and tobacco. They can't take care of their children and . . . they run down all the nice communities. Black people cause all the problems of the world, everyone knows that. Why they don't even own the ghettos that they live in. The truth is that they want what white folk have honestly earned; education, beachfront property, homes in the suburbs, businesses, good paying jobs and even equal voting rights . . . Most of them can't even read. I'm not a racist, I've never harmed a black person in my entire life. I say, the color of a man's skin doesn't matter."

These were the words of an enslaved black man, in America, in the sixties, in the ghetto and he was not alone in his opinion.

There was the perception that the average white males say nothing. They just go on with their lives stepping on who ever stands in their path, white, black, yellow or red, it matters not. Their paths lead to success in America. They are the men with the most; the biggest and the best. No man woman or child can stand in his way. He has or gets what everyone wants and if you don't want what he has he'll put his down and take yours . . . your respect, your woman, the admiration of your children and even the love of your God.

PART ONE

Chapter 1

"Yo-lept, yo-lept, yo-lept" was the mock military cadence being called out on a wintry March night. The windy air was filled with an icy drizzle mixed with snow flurries. One after another, each sad shivering and frightened teenage face filed by. Each covered with elements of winter that stuck to the fronts of their entire bodies. Marching in unison they turned towards their destination, an old auditorium being used as a theater. A barely visible light above lit the way along the eight-foot ice covered walkway. The ground on each side of the side walk was covered with a half-foot or more of previously fallen snow. It was most definitely a nasty day or rather . . . a nasty night.

Just ahead and an equal distance behind there were lines of boys six abreast in-groups of forty. They were all dressed alike in brown summer like denim blazers and wool hats. Most had their collars turned up to their ears and their chins held close against their chest. In Jackson's group, every hand was tucked deep into their pockets in an attempt to keep warm on this night's trek to the weekly picture show. This was Jackson's first night here. At age fourteen, this is not where he or anyone that loved him; hoped he would be. The wet dreary weather had no meaning to him. All he had in his heavy hanging heart were questions and pleads.

"God, Momma, please, please come and take me home; I want, I need to be home. I'll never, and I mean never do it again. Please," he kept repeating,

"What did I do? U'm not a bad person, u'm not, u'm just not."

He had to be very concerned that someone may see him crying. Inconspicuously, he used the cuff of his sleeve and wiped away a stream of tears that had trickled down his blemish free handsome young face. He was young and very proud. If it were possible he would have turned back the hands of time and try to be different. He would try to be smart instead of adventurous. Anything, at this moment he would do any thing, to get back to his humble home with his four siblings.

He lifted his head and briefly glanced back over his left shoulder to see if his friend El-Tez was okay.

"Eyes forward," Shouted a loud cruel voice of authority. His quick momentary backward glance exposed many faces and they all seemed to have the same frightful expression. Hidden under the freezing drizzle each boy wore the tears of fear and heartbreak.

"I'm scared," Jackson whispered much too low for anyone else to hear.

"I am so scared." Far up ahead the boys were older and seemly much bigger. At the very front they were striding with a rhythm indicating no fear. They stomped their feet on the slushy pavement right in time with the cadence. They had become accustom to this marching routine and apparently learned to do it with style and cockiness. Suddenly, from the ranks came another roaring voice of authority,

"Get your ass back in line!" Once more it rang out, this time much louder than the single voice of the cadence caller and this time with a new sense of urgency.

"Get back in line! Get back here!" he shouted as several young white boys broke the formation and headed down over a nearby hillside.

"Everyone stop, don't move! Tom go back and call security, we've got three runners. Everyone else keep your groups in line! Get'm turned around!" he commanded. Voices of command were now being shouted by all of the security guards that had been marching along side of the young juvenile prisoners. The intensity was getting thick enough to reach out and grab by the hands-full and it was building by the minute in both the guards and the youths.

This is Morganza, a place for bad and uncontrollable youths. This is the place that every young boy feared. The place where it had long been rumored that one had to, 'fight or lose your virginity'. The place ruled by Philadelphia's street gangs. The place where most white boys and many smaller more timid boys could easily become victims of rape or even killed, just for being vulnerable.

"God, please let me go home, I'll never do it again." Jackson continued and repeated to himself again and again as the frenzy for freedom heightened.

Chapter 2

In the world outside of the perimeters of Morganza, it was just another night. A few weeks earlier a juvenile court judge had sentenced Jackson Thomas, age fourteen, of Bethel Park to an indefinite period of time to the Western Pennsylvania Training Institute for boys, better known as Morganza. Jackson was one of six responsible for a string of store burglaries that had been committed over a two year period by an organized ring of four juveniles calling themselves the 409. Their ages were fourteen through seventeen. Two adults, ages twenty-four and twenty-six, were also arrested and awaiting trial in the criminal courts. Jackson Thomas, the youngest of the ring and considered the ring leader, was charged with forty two known burglaries and master minding the break-in of South Hills Sears Roebuck Department Store, in which thousands of dollars worth of jewelry and small appliances were taken. A reward had been offered for information leading to the arrest of the burglar or burglars responsible for the theft.

The reward was given to a neighbor, a sixteen-year old friend of the group who on occasion, was taken along as a comrade in crime. His family was considered poorer than the rest of them involved and it was obvious that they needed the money. In 1959 an average yearly salary in this small coal mining community was less than four thousand dollars. It was understood why he snitched. The family had no father in the household or any means of income. They, just as many other poor families, lived month to month depending upon the surplus food provided from the Welfare Department. Every month families received five pounds of American cheese, five pounds of sugar, a pound of butter, peanut-butter, spam and a few other food items that were meant to sustain a family from month to month. Even so . . . no matter how tough life was, there was no place in a gang for a snitch. They were all enraged enough to make a pact that they would someday get Pooh-Pooh for his squealing.

There were four of them thus the name they chose. The name was 'The 409,' picked by Jackson because of his uncle that fought in the Korean War and he always spoke of his black platoon nick-named the 409. Jackson's best friend, Eddie Brooks was sixteen, he was convicted and sentenced to 2-5 years at Camp Hill, which was supposedly the worst young adult institution in the state of Pennsylvania. The typical age at Camp Hill was between seventeen and twenty five. In 1961 it was considered a hole at the bottom of hell, even to the worst criminals. The only white boy in the gang, Billy Muldon, was sentenced to the custody of his parents and one year probation. He had quote, "just gotten involved with the wrong group of boys."

A fourteen-year old, nick named, El-Tez was also sentenced to Morganza. The two adults involved were ultimately found guilty of receiving stolen goods and contributing to the delinquency of a minor, namely Billy Muldon; and were both sentenced to 2-5 years in the Western Penitentiary.

"Stop you stupid asses, you can't get away!" The three boys that broke rank weren't about to listen. They were already down over the hill and running like scared rabbits with no one in pursuit. Only the screaming voices of the twelve or so guards kept some order in the remaining group of prisoners. They would not dare leave their groups to chase a few runaways.

"Jackson" from all of the confusion; came the voice of El-Tez who had been walking directly behind Jackson.

"Um go'na run, I don't wan'a be here, I can't take it man, um scared." El-Tez, real name, Ronald Allen, was older than Jackson. He was born and raised, until the age of twelve, in Coatesville Pa., where he often found himself unwanted and usually in some kind of trouble. He was very light complexioned and had some how manage to get one of his front teeth knocked out at an early age. He had a little early teenage peach fuzz above his lips that added a break in his other wise light skin. El-Tez, like Jackson, wore a processed hair style that had turned a tint of red as a result of the lye and soap mixture that was used by blacks to straighten hair in the early sixties. He was nice looking, but kind of fidgety. He always looked as if he were going to break out running at any given moment. His love for his comrades and Jackson was unquestioned.

"No man, don't run, we don't know where we would be going," Jackson responded.

By now the sudden and electrifying sounds of pushing and stomping were surging from every sector of the crowd of new coming prisoners. One after another the boys began to break rank and run for their freedom. A few of the youths were grabbed and wrestled to the ground by guards just as they started to make their break. Meanwhile El-Tez repeated,

"Please Jackson, um-go'n, come on with me, please" he suddenly darted from the crowd. Jackson reached for El-Tez' in an effort to pull him back in line but instead he was instantly running beside him. In a matter of seconds Jackson found himself fifty or more feet away from the group.

"We messed up," Jackson started repeating to himself as he ran stride for stride with El-Tez. He had the strange feeling that everything in the peripheral darkness around him accelerate each time he stretch one leg in front of the other. Ignoring the icy sleet that was relentlessly smacking against his face, he went on knowing there could be no turning back now.

Every boy that ran had some how gathered into one mass of running people. They ran blindly, relying upon whoever was just ahead to lead the way. Like a herd of stampeding buffalo they recklessly descended the hillside, tripping, falling and quickly getting back up onto their feet without losing a step. Jackson became aware of the sounds of his own body panting hard and wheezing with every intake of oxygen. Dumbfounded he continued, at times closing his eyes completely and relying solely on his instinct to deliver each falling foot step.

The yelling voice of authority could now faintly be heard. Pains began to strike at his side. His breathing puffed away from his nostrils like a locomotive, causing his chest to swell and deflate faster and faster.

"We messed up," Jackson continued to mumble. El-Tez suddenly stumbled over something or someone in his path. His legs quickly became entangled with Jackson's causing both of them to tumble downward over a heavily scrubbed embankment. Jackson held his eyes tightly closed trying to avoid anything that may cause injury as they fell through breaking branches and briers. After a few seconds every noise around them finally and abruptly stopped . . . Jackson lay still for a few moments on the banks of a creek that encircled the entire Morganza complex. Six or seven youths had gathered nearby contemplating just how they were going to get across and complete their get away. The creek looked to be about forty feet wide. The water current was swift with remnants of ice formed along the shoreline. Jackson had just stood up when and a sharp pain called his attention to his right leg. So much adrenaline flow prevented his pain from being a concern, at least for the moment.

"Let's do it," someone yelled, referring to their intentions of jumping into the stream of ice-cold water. Jackson was one of several who choose the head first diving method of entering the water. Others leaped in butt first in anticipation of standing upright once they were in the water as opposed to the possibility of swimming across. In the mist of all the turmoil, humor found its way into what had turned into a momentary calamity. In the night-light they had not determined just how deep the water was. In the non-thinking moment of escape, everyone hit the water at nearly the same time. As said, they leaped headfirst and butt-first from the embankment, which was about three feet higher than the water surface. The water turned out to be only about three inches deep at the point of entry, causing the would be deep water splashes to be no splash at all and a lot of hard thumping sounds of bodies striking the shallow creek bottom.

"Shit," someone blurted out, as unexpected laughter filled the night air. The laughter was brief as everyone scrambled and clawed their way back onto their feet. Soaked and wet, and now torn and bruised, their quest for freedom could not afford to pause too long for that one moment of humor.

Lying on the creek bottom with excruciating pains jolting from every part of his body, Jackson screamed out in agony. The contact with the creek bottom at the angle of his dive caused him to badly scrape both elbows. His chest had dragged along the rocky bottom tearing through his clothing and gashing him. His left nipple was hanging by a piece of flesh. His blood became distinguishable even in the dark. The water was so shallow that most of his back remained dry. Those who were not injured were back onto their feet and proceeding into the deeper part of the creek. They dog paddled across in their continued quest for the other shore.

Jackson sat back on the bank of the Morganza side of the creek, trying to make some decision on what to do next. Suddenly, there was nothing but silence. He listened for any sound that had filled the cold night air just a few moments ago. He heard only the trickling sound of the creek, no voices, no splashing, and no screaming guards.

"I'm alone. Dam-it I'm all alone," he whispered. About eight feet to his left, in shallow water, someone was lying face down. It appeared to be El-Tez.

"El-Tez are you all right?" Grabbing his own leg, Jackson felt what he thought to be a piece of branch protruding through his flesh. He attempted to pull it out as if it were a splinter, only to go back into excruciating pain after realizing that it felt like it was a piece of his own leg that had exited through his pants. The injury had resulted from the initial fall against the embankment.

"El-Tez" His voice was now pleading, trying to get attention "are you all right?" Still silence, El-Tez was not moving. After dragging himself closer he reached and grabbed El-Tez by the cuff of his pants and pulled him out of the shallow water still lying face down.

"Oh God, he's dead," Jackson dramatically cried out loudly. He leaned back against the ground and looked upward into the snowy sleet and called out to God in fear, but in mind only.

God please come, I need you bad, I'm so, so sorry. He had yet to make a sound or to yell for help from someone that may still be around. His pleading to God was beginning to be repetitious. He, meaning God, was not coming, neither was momma or anyone else.

I'm not afraid to die, but I am afraid of being alone in the dark and I always have been. Now I'm in the dark, alone, freezing cold, a broken leg, a nearly severed nipple and . . . a dead friend lying at my feet. On top of all this, this fellow God, that everyone speaks so highly of, is no where to be found. Oh momma, momma, momma.

Jackson began to quietly doze off to sleep. It was getting colder and colder by the minute. It wasn't long before ice began to form around his eyes and lips. In the comforting mind-set of surrendering his soul to what ever was to come next, he curled up his body and yielded to unconsciousness. He had decided to give up and to lie there and die beside his friend. Oh momma, were words poised upon his lips as he drifted back into his relevant past.

No longer was he lying helpless on the cold grounds of Morganza. His vivid memory grabbed him by the heart and took him back to a time that had played a major part in the creation of his own character. Faint voices of his second grade school mates came alive in his mind. Without understanding how, he was back in the nearly all white school that he had attended as a child.

"Pay attention!" screamed the teacher. She had caught him gazing out of the window instead of paying attention to instruction. After several warnings, she, being annoyed by his short attention span, blatantly informed him of how repulsive he was to her and that he was a good example of why colored people should not be put in the same environment as whites; because of their inability to learn.

"In fact," she calmly said, "as a lesson to you and the other children in class, turn your desk around towards the window that you're always looking out of so you may learn from what you see and not interfere with those who belong here. Go head, I said, do it right now."

Feeling slighted but quite content with his new seating arrangement, he let his daydreaming ability take him in and out of the classroom. Occasionally when something of interest to him was being discussed and caught his attention, he turned his head toward her to listen and play apart. She caught him looking and once again screamed as if someone was stealing something. She made a quick pointing gesture indicating he should look back outside and not at her. She gave him pencils and paper and told him not to disturb her class again, "if you do," she said "you are going right to the principal's office."

Recess and outdoor activities could not come quickly enough. During his lonely time during class, he found himself sketching and drawing pictures from his imagination of super heroes and cartoon characters. There were times each day that he remembered paying attention to her instructions without looking towards the front of the class for fear she would make a spectacle of him and his world of contentment with his own class within the class. He found himself passing every test and always managing to get a passing grade in spite of his disgruntled teacher. This infuriated her even more. Once again, she caught him looking at her while she was giving instructions.

"What are you looking at?" she asked. "You're repulsive and I can't teach this class with your interruptions." She grabbed him by the earlobe, lifted him from his chair and led him to the principal's office. Upon entering she said; "this boy was being disobedient and disruptive in class". The tall thin white principal easily believed the accusation.

"Is this true Mr. Thomas?" he sarcastically asked. He walked over to his office closet and brought out a wooden paddle and began to slap it against his own hand while walking back towards Jackson.

"Are you causing trouble in the classroom Mr. Thomas?" Jackson shook his head, no.

"Are you calling your teacher a liar then?" Jackson again shook his head from side to side.

"Speak up boy are you calling Ms. Dickson a liar?"

"No" was Jackson's answer.

"I see . . . so then . . . you are disrupting the class like she says. What do you think we should do about this?" Jackson was confused by the question and simply hunched his shoulders as if to say, I don't know.

"You don't know? Well, maybe I can show you. In fact I'm going to show you and all the other students what happens to a little nigger boy that causes trouble in class or any where else. I'm going to make an example of you. Do you know what that means?" Jackson again shook his head from side to side. The principal turned on the intercom speaker system and made an announcement.

"This is your principal speaking. I want all of you to know that what you are about to hear is the sound of Jackson Thomas getting what he deserves. This is what happens when you act stupid in class and backtalk your teacher." He gestured for Jackson to bend over. Jackson hesitated and he immediately grabbed him by the arm and pushed him down over the arm of a chair. He then commenced what he called 'a good hard lesson with the paddle.' The paddle was slammed hard against Jackson's rear end, once . . . twice . . . and again for good measure. In Jackson's mind he could hear the loud laughter from all of the children throughout the school. Though it had happen long ago, the anger stirred Jackson to a point that even now he nearly regained consciousness from his dream.

After a few stirring seconds back into the reality of the night, he again drifted back into his past, again finding himself sitting back at his desk that was now turned completely around and facing the rear of the class. There he remained . . . perfectly still for what seemed to be a very, very, long time. The laughter of the classmates was faint and seemingly coming from miles away. His stubborn character and what he thought was their limited ability to muster genuine affection or understanding for a colored boy, was causing him to boil inside. What he had managed to learn in the classroom was virtually self-taught. In his reality he thought that everyone was self-taught or learned from life's experience. His father had imprinted many lessons that were born out of a type of affection that warranted all the praise his young mind could generate. He recalled when his father had told him of a time when the only education a black man needed to achieve and be successful down in Alabama was to complete third grade and the famous three 'r's, 'reading, riting and rithmetic.' He recalled that his older brother dreamed of completing the ninth grade to get onto his road to success. Jackson was encouraged to at least get his G. E. D. This was a time in Jackson's young life when he listen to the voices around him, what folks thought of him, compared to what he thought of himself. What he meant to them; who meant something to him; who's willing to live without him. He heard some good white folk calling him a common criminal, he didn't think so. The good black folk saw him as a troublemaker, he didn't feel that way. His peers sometimes called him crazy, he thought he was brave . . . His friends thought of him as a comrade they could count on; He lived up to the expectations. His younger siblings believed he could do no wrong; that he was an adventurer. His mother said 'Not my baby'. His father always said, 'That's my boy'. There were others without comment; to him they were the mannequins of life; no thoughts, no voice, just taking up space where they will always remain. His dad that raised him was his god; a black man with limited use of his left arm. He worked from four a.m. until well after sun down; seven days of the week. With one arm he could achieve more than most men with two. He was more capable of affection for children that weren't his own, than others could muster for their own. He never attended church to Jackson's knowledge. He never attended bars or after hour joints like those who attended church. He never spoke out against different life styles. He taught by example. He always seemed to focus on the abundance of affection and avoided conflicts that came with jealousy and minding other folks business. To Jackson he was a real man. Jackson often thought to himself, 'I would like to have only one arm so my dad and I could be alike; me and my dad, building garages and room additions with two arms, his right and my left. What a couple of comrades we would be. Jackson honored this man who had a total of seven children; a man who always reflected warmth and security for each and every one of them. Jackson could not remember much about his biological father in his younger years. He knew he had another father by folks saying that, 'he looks just like his real daddy', every chance they got. Jackson usually ignored them and honestly didn't know or care what they were talking about.

A gear shifted in Jackson's mind and placed him at around the age of five. He heard his daddy, 'Chuck', call his older brother Larry, to the kitchen of the old two bedroom home with an outhouse toilet built by Sears Roebuck in the 1930's, where he was sitting nearby enjoying the sweet smell of his mother's blackberry cobbler and listening to the Amos and Andy show on the radio. Jackson heard his daddy tell Larry that he needed something from the shed out back and wanted Larry to get it for him. Larry, being about fourteen at the time, waited patiently for instructions on what and where it was that his daddy wanted. Jackson wanted to be recognized and wondered why his dad didn't just send him instead of Larry. Jackson seen himself lighting out the back door heading for the shed as fast as he could run . . . yep, he left Larry far behind, this was his big opportunity to serve the man that served them so well . . . he thought. Down the old wooden steps he ran, up the rear path and into the shed that was connected to the outhouse. This was the earliest act of self-inflicted disappointment that he could remember in his life. He had yet to learn the importance of being instructed properly, the value of patience or the advantage of clarity. He only knew, he had to act fast and not let this opportunity go by. So, there he stood . . . the first one in the shed, in the dark, without a light and not knowing what he had come to get or even where it might be. Larry finally came into the shed with a light, looked on a shelf, got a screwdriver and walked back to the house with Jackson following sadly and disappointedly behind. As Larry handed the screwdriver to their daddy, Jackson quietly walked pass trying not to be noticed. He had missed a big chance to shine; the chance to give something back. His dad, being the man that he was, noticed his sadness and by now, his trickle of tears and called him back into the kitchen. "Son," he said, "I want you to go and get me . . ." Jackson grabbed the flashlight and headed for the door again as fast as lightning. This time his daddy caught him. "Wait, wait, Jackson, let me tell you what I want son". "Oh", Jackson said while panting like a thorough-bred horse waiting for the starting gate to open. Jackson momentarily halted with his feet still pointed towards the door. "I want you to get me a pair of grip-pliers". Like a bat out of hell he was gone again. If Larry had tried to go along he would have fought him like the devil. Back into the shed he went. This time with a flashlight; this time, knowing what he was there for; this time knowing that it was in the toolbox. He opened the box while breathing hard from the short sprint and believing that how quickly he could return would make him look better than Larry. 'Oh God', he thought, 'I don't know what grip-pliers look like. I see pliers, screwdrivers, wrenches and plenty of other unidentified things.' He quietly sat on the floor of the shed with the toolbox at his side, frustrated by his own lack of knowledge. After a few moments he dozed off to sleep, waking only as he realized that he was against the chest of his dad and being carried back into the house. Jackson some how knew that he would someday get another chance. He knew this man understood. At the age of five he had learned the first and vital steps to being educated. First, decide what it is you want; second, identify it's importance, what it looks like, its worth to you and those you love; third, find out where it is and how to get there, identify the competition, anticipate the obstacles and prepare for the unexpected. Fourth-learn patience, get clarity and understanding before you set out on your journey. Know that you don't have to be first, just do it the best that you can; and last but not least, know that if you ever fail and someone loves you, they will be there to carry you to safety. Start all over again and someday you will be smart enough to carry someone else to safety just as you were carried; all this makes your education worth while. His dad knew what his tools were worth, where they were located, how they were used, their value and the feeling of ownership. In such a simple lesson, he taught as a teacher should, that 'lessons aren't always learned on a schedule'. He taught him that 'there is a reward for trying' and that, 'it's all right to not know as much as all others'. At the end of the lesson he understood that there would be another day. In closing the lesson he taught that, 'failing wasn't as important as trying. There can be just as much love for those who fail as those who succeed. "That's my boy, he's got a good heart," he heard his father tell his mother on that night.

Just as the intrusion of peace and tranquility was completed a lightning bolt of pain again exploded in Jackson's right leg. Startled, he woke from his dream-like visit to his past and lifted up into a sitting position. 'This is not the time to give up', he thought, 'my dad and family back home love me and need to know that I'm strong enough to confront any worldly thing to assure them of my love in return. I've got to get up'. He crawled up the embankment and back onto the upward grade from which he had come a short while ago.

Dragging himself upright and onto his one good leg, he made his way back out onto the open field. Jackson hadn't realized how far they had run in that mad dash for freedom. He could faintly see through the now heavily falling snow. The lights of the huge administration building were looming at the center of the complex just about a quarter of a mile from where he stood. There was no one in sight. No search lights, guards, or dogs . . . nothing. It was as if this were all a dream or that he was the only piece of reality caught in the mist of someone else's nightmare.

He slowly made his way up towards the only building in sight. Even in the cold he had began to sweat causing chills to run the whole gamut of his body. He would not give up this time. He wanted to live; he wanted to grow to be just as good as or maybe even a better man than his god-like father.

He found himself slumped to the ground within feet from a huge green door located under a main colonial entryway above. He had given his all. There was not another ounce of strength left in his body. He tried to reach out just once more. Just as his reach fell short of the base of the door a nun pulled it open from the inside and immediately began to assist him.

Caringly, she and another pulled him up onto his feet and into a nearby chair and softly said, "wait right there". After a few moments he dozed off as a result of complete fatigue. He thought he was again dreaming as two different nuns appeared standing over him and seemingly surprised to find him sitting inside the corridor. They recognized that his leg had been injured and lifted him by his shoulders asking;

"How did you get in here?"

"The other two nuns brought me in," Jackson answered.

"There are no other nuns here young man," one of them responded. "How did you get that old door open? It's been jammed shut for years and no one ever uses it."

"But they did, they picked me up and brought me inside"

"Young man, there are no other nuns here," she repeated.

"But there was" he said. "There really was" he said again.

"Well they must have been angels" she said in a kidding tone of voice. Jackson wondered and stayed silent as they led him away.

They escorted him down to a lower level to an infirmary. He didn't utter another word about his life saving 'other nuns', and they, in return, did not ask another question. Jackson slowly began to regain a stronger sense of consciousness.

The brightly lit narrow room with metal benches extending from wall to wall on both sides, helped bring him into total awareness. Out of thirty or so boys that had broken rank to run, twenty-six, himself included, were quietly sitting with their heads hung and just like him they were soaked and shivering. They had been disrobed, showered and wrapped in military blankets while waiting to be taken back to the intake cottage from were they had ran no more than two hours ago. Three guards entered through a rear door on the far side of the room and were quietly looking and gesturing to the boys as if not wanting to wake or disturb anyone else in the building. Those that were injured were simply told to wait there until the physician arrived.

All toll, four escaped, four were injured, a total of twenty-six were returned to custody and Jackson knew that one of the four did not escape, El-Tez lie dead down near the creek.

Chapter 3

Visitation rules were one visit per month, no visit for the first sixty days. Any violations of cottage rules resulted in a lost of visitation privileges. For his attempt to escape there would be no visiting privilege for Jackson Thomas until June. All new comers were assigned to the intake cottage number five, for a period of ninety days before being reassigned to a cottage in the general population. Your cottage assignment was based on your age and behavior during your first ninety days of incarceration. The racial make up of number-five cottage was about fifty-fifty, with most of the youth being from the Philadelphia area. The remaining boys were from all over Pennsylvania, including Pittsburgh and Harrisburg. A large percentage of the Morganza population had never committed a crime of any kind. They were moved from institution to institution based on their age. Some were abandoned children that had not been adopted and were simply moved into the juvenile system. Others had parents that had passed away or they were simply runaways. Of those sentenced for crimes, most were there for auto theft and petty thefts, like shoplifting. The large number of the boys was sentenced from of Philadelphia for gang related charges.

After the great attempted escape, the daily routines of a boy's home began to take shape. Jackson's sixty-day stay at the intake cottage was what one might call 'an introduction to a harsh reality'. Like many of the other youngsters being introduced to an environment without affection, he longed to be with the folk back home. Jackson was continuously kept at a high level of fear. He constantly wished that it would all go away or that his momma would find away to get him back home.

Upon his arrival to the number five intake cottage, the population was brought to attention for the purpose of introducing an incoming group of five including Jackson. After the introduction, he was assigned to an eating table for six, which would become his permanent seat until he was moved into general population.

"Can I have your meat?" what a strange question, it was being asked by a seventeen year old boy that stood about six feet three inches in height and weighing about two hundred fifteen pounds. Both sides of his head were bald and scared from what appeared to be burns. Jackson was later informed that, Mohigan, real name Lee Dorsey, was held over an open oven burner by his mother and burned severely on both sides of his face. After he lost consciousness his mother purposely set the house on fire. He was left inside the blazing home in an attempt to murder him for an insurance claim. Fortunately or unfortunately, he survived the fire and was put up for adoption at the age of four. Because of the scars he was never adopted. After years of being institutionalized, molested, raped and abused, he ended up in Morganza. Now he was sitting in front of thirteen year-old Jackson, very big, very strong and very hateful.

"Yea," was Jackson's answer, though he wanted the slice of meat loaf more than he'd ever know, yet, he raked it from his own plate onto his. In the dining room no one was permitted to talk. All conversation, if any, was at a whisper. Jackson quickly gobbled his potatoes and beans. He didn't want Mohigan to think for a moment that he wasn't hungry.

"Do you want that cake?"

"No, you can have it," damn, he wanted that cake so bad he thought, while sliding it beside the other five pieces Mohigan already had. Jackson had thought it was strange that when he first sat down, everyone at the table slid their cake to Mohigan. For a brief moment Mohigan stopped eating and looked directly at Jackson. He perched his lips as if throwing a kiss and made a kissing sound directed to Jackson. 'Oh no', Jackson thought while slightly shaking his head. He wanted to throw up what little he had eaten. He had never heard of a boy throwing a kiss to a boy. In fact, at that time he didn't know it was possible to be sexually active with the same sex in any way, or how or why anyone would want to be. Mohigan leaned toward him and purposely brushed his nasty lips against Jackson's ear.

"Tell Mr. Blake you want to be roomed in the center wing, I'll make sure that no one bothers you", he whispered and winked at the same time.

'Momma please get me home, I'll never do anything wrong again in my life . . . please, Jackson thought to himself. He hadn't been taught much about praying and the prayers he had been accustomed to were prayers like, 'get me a new football' or 'please protect my brothers and sisters', or at most 'please don't let momma whoop me'. Since he arrived there, he prayed every chance he got. 'I'm so lost, let it be a dream, please God, send me home and what ever you do please don't send me to center wing'.

"Everyone go to the recreation room, except for the kitchen detail, quietly do it now," Mr. Blake demanded. Mr. Blake was a stocky middle aged man that did not take any back talk from anyone. What he had to say he said once and showed it the second time with force. The evening guard shift consisted of two men. Dinner time was over at 5:30. Everyone was allowed three hours of recreation time to play ping-pong, checkers, and dominos or hit the punching bags. The punching bags part stuck in Jackson's mind. 'Why would there be a need for punching bags?'

Once in the recreation room, the guards usually locked them in and returned up to the main floor to listen to a ball game or just chat with each other until it was time to lock down for bed, leaving the youths to whatever they choose to do inside the one big locked down room unsupervised. At 8:30 p.m., the boys were assigned a shower time of ten minutes, lined up for a group prayer and led to the sleeping quarters on the third floor. The third floor consisted of three wings; each wing had approximately ten metal bunk beds to sleep twenty youth each. Once checked into your bunk and counted you weren't allowed to talk, leave your bed or go to the rest room. Each wing was locked down separately until morning at which time you'd receive a work order. If you did not receive a work order, you'd go directly to the recreation room until called for daily meals.

"Where you from?" a friendly voice, this was a surprise.

"Pittsburgh" Jackson answered.

"What part?"

"I'm from out by South Park, a place called Coverdale."

"I heard of that, we used to go out there and dance at the Barn. Listen home-boy; don't let these guys from Philly run over you. You shouldn't even be here at your age. If you let'm they're gon'na make you a girl." While he continued to talk, Jackson was stuck on how in the world he could possibly become a girl. He continued on. "They'll take your outside gifts or what ever they want from you. I'm just telling you to watch your back. There are six other guys from the Burg," he went on saying. "That light skinned guy at the checker table," he said as he pointed, "His name is Wesley White, he's from the Hill. The guy he's playing is Melvin, he's from Homewood. Those four dudes talking by the window, they're all from Schenley. They're part of the Cherokee Gang. I can't remember their names but they're alright. I heard your one of the ones that tried to run, what happen?"

"I don't know, we just ran, we almost made it, (that is what Jackson's dad always called 'lying for no reason,') "but the creek was too deep and just to many policemen."

"You guys must-a-been crazy, cold as it was and you're a thousand miles from the Burg."

Jackson hadn't mentioned to anyone about El-Tez. He assumed they think he got away and they haven't found his body yet. When I get my first visit I'm going to tell my mom. She will know what to do, I hope, Jackson thought.

"What the f—you looking at?" a Philadelphia gang boy ask Jackson, and gave him an evil eye.

"Nothing," Jackson answered.

"You call'n me noth'n, fool?"

"No man."

"You bet'not, I'll mess up your pretty face."

"Leave'm alone man, he ain't said noth'n to you," said Jackson's newly found homeboy.

"What'chu got to do wit it? I'll mess you up too."

"It ain't dare, you ain't do'n noth'n to me."

The Philly boy quickly came over to the Pittsburgh boy that had been talking to Jackson. He paused and stepped back into a boxing stance gesturing Jackson's newly found homeboy into a boxing match. Homeboy looked down at the floor for a second and then back at Jackson. With out warning he turned and laid a sucker punch to the head of the Philly boy who was caught totally off guard. The Philly boy took the blow and tried to return a punch of his own only to find himself briefly on the shoulders of homeboy and then instantly slammed to the floor and being kicked. Homeboy was screaming down at him "don't mess with me you jive fagot." As sudden as he had hit the floor three others boys from Philly had jumped in throwing a barrage of punches at the Pittsburgh boy. He tried to hold his own but he was over come by so many blows.

Jackson wanted to help but his heart wouldn't let him. He didn't know what to do. The guards, hearing and recognizing the ruckus, quickly appeared and broke up the fight.

"Any more fighting your going to the hole, that means all of you."

"They started it," said a wimpy voice coming from Jackson's mouth.

"Shut up and sit down, if there's going to be fight'n it'll be at the bags or both winner and loser goes to the hole for a week." With that, both guards re-locked the door and went back up stairs. Homeboy looked at Jackson in disappointment.

"You ain't got no heart, um out of it," he said as he turned and walked away leaving Jackson on his own. There was nothing Jackson could say. He had disappointed himself more than any one else. 'I'm a punk; I just want to go home.' As usual his words were just his own thoughts. The stares and glares were passing around the room as homeboy walked away to an area where the other Pittsburgh boys had gathered, leaving Jackson alone on the wrong side of the room.

After the recreation room gate was closed and locked, Jackson watched as the guards hurried to get back up the stairs to continue whatever they were doing. 'Don't they realize there's a crisis'? Jackson was leaning against the metal gate wishing that he could be with El-Tez while still praying that some how he would suddenly awaken and find himself back home in Coverdale.

A ping-pong ball was being slapped back and forth by two white boys who were trying very hard to mind their own business. Jackson was trying his best not to look at anyone in the room. He imagined that he must have been wearing the saddest face possible. The seven Pittsburgh boys seemed to be miles away gathered and standing closely together with their backs facing the walls. Homeboy was still bleeding and dabbing a cloth to his lips while never taking his eyes off of a Philly group of about twenty-two boys that had gathered across the room. The Philly boys were talking. Five or six of them were lightly jabbing and weaving at each other as if preparing to enter into a boxing-match. Jackson later learned that these twenty or so Philly boys were all from one gang. Out on the street they were called the 'Valley'. Most of the gangs in Philly were named after the street corners in the areas they resided in, examples being Commack and Norris, Vine Street, Deuce, etc. Others had names like Rollers, Tender lions and the Vice. In the institutions across Pennsylvania they stood united in a bigger way. All of the gangs from North Philly formed a truce with South Philly, and West Philly did the same. The Valley was a part of South Philly.

After doing their ritual of preparing for an in-house gang war they began to stride towards the Pittsburgh boys encircling them in the far corner away from Jackson. "What's up Big Sam;" came a voice from another side of the room. Big Sam was a huge dark skinned boy who hadn't played a part in the first melee. He was what the Philly boys called a 'Head'. He was obligated by a gang pledge to lead his gang to war. Sam glanced and gave his gang sign to another named Spider. It was an indication of war and for him to stay out of what was about to go down. Spider was a major gang leader of the Tender Lions of North Philly and seemed to know that the codes of street war applied even in confinement. He stood up gave his gang sign and approached the area where the Sam's gang was starting to posture. When Spider stood, so did another eight of his corner boys from different locations throughout the room. They recognized his gang-signal as one of their own. Spider was a tall lean light skinned boy of about seventeen, slightly hunched backed, with a Hispanic accent. He was not nearly as big as Big Sam, but he was well known on the street and out in the Morganza population as a high ranking gang leader of the largest gang in Philadelphia.

"This is not the place to call for war," he said looking directly in Sam's face as if daring him to challenge his authority.

"We'll all go to the hole for thirty days, and I ain't into that right now. Plus your boy got his ass kicked straight up. I'm call'n for a fair," Spider said. In Philly a 'fair' was a fair match between an equal number of boys or one on one.

"The young boy on the rail started it, give him a fair and let's end this," Spider said while pointing directly at Jackson. He added, "you," meaning the homeboy from Pittsburgh, "I don't want to see no more jack-up shit. You got'ta straight-up box on a fair or we ain't side'n, solid?"

"Solid," came the response from homeboy, he was seemingly relieved that he may not have to fight again on this day.

"Who you got Sam?" asked Spider. Sam scanned his boys and asked them,

"Who wants to mess him up," he said, while gesturing over at Jackson with a nod of his head. They all seemed to chuckle, as if Jackson was more pathetic than he felt. One big lipped boy with a southern draw responded and said, "I got'm." His street name was, Little John. He looked like a Big John to Jackson. He was about two hundred forty pounds with an average shaped. He had beady eyes, 'kind of like that of a snake' Jackson thought. They called him little because his head looked to small for his body. At thirteen Jackson had just began to grow into what they called a country boy. He was light skinned, against his wishes, curly haired, nearly six feet tall and very big boned. He had broad shoulders and weighed about two hundred and fifteen pounds. In better times back home he was always grinning and filled with life and, mischievousness. He had been in school fights back home but mostly they wrestled until someone said 'I give' and the other kid was declared the winner. No blood, nothing broken, maybe a scratch or two, but that was an event where he came from.

When Little John reached the point of standing smack in front of Jackson he put his fist up in a boxing manner. Everyone from Philly seemed to know how to box. It is said that, 'there's a pal boxing gym on nearly every corner of Philly', to help keep kids off the street. Where Jackson was from back in Coverdale, catching snakes and exploring wooded areas was a calling.

None the less, there he stood with his hands at his side trying to disappear before he was hit. His mind raddled off the same old silent prayer, 'Momma please, God please, somebody, somewhere do something.' Out loud Jackson muttered, "I don't wan' a fight." Looking into Jackson's eyes Little John simply said without expression or pity, "Come on." He was barely peaking over his left fist as he jabbed Jackson lightly in the mouth. Jackson put one hand in his pocket and held the other up and cupped open almost in surrender. His eyes were focused towards the floor in a submissive way. He was scared and did not want to be hurt nor did he have any desire to hurt anyone else.

"I don't want to fight." he repeated. Bop, was the sound of another left jab that found Jackson's mouth again. The last punch was harder than the first. He could taste his own blood as his teeth had cut into his inner lip but he still remained submissive. Boom, boom, boom, three full force punches landed against Jackson's broad chest, rocking him back onto the hills of his feet and back against the gate. Jackson looked around pathetically hoping for help from somebody, in this case anybody.

"Come on" little John repeated as he punched his own chest with a light left and right and then a quick slap to Jackson's face. Jackson had had enough; he removed his hand from his pocket and put his chin against his own chest. He closed his eyes and gritted his teeth in anger and in fear. Jackson yelled as loud as he could, "I said I don't want to fight!" He was swinging his fist wildly in blind fury. "Leave me alone!" Though he was yelling to be left alone every blow he threw was finding its mark. His punches were landing, first to his opponent's chest and then to his forehead and back down to his chest again. Nothing came back. Jackson opened his eyes and recognized the look of shock upon the face of Little John. Little John began to back up with an expression of shock as blood suddenly poured from his nose. Jackson began to imitate what he had seen Little John do with his hands. He actually stood in a boxing stance as if his cowardly acts were a part of a deception. Now it was Jackson's turn. It was he who blurted out, "come-on." He began to feel the adrenalin of victory. Little John was hurt and ready to quit.

"Cut," someone said cut.

'What the hell is cut, was Jackson's thought. Apparently, cut meant that in a 'fair', if your corner boy is losing you can step in as if it were a dance. In came another Valley boy name Duce. He was shorter than Little John but he was much broader. His boxing style was different. He crouched way down and threw punches from a squatted position. Two punches came to Jackson, no damage. Jackson returned with one punch sending Duce to the floor and out like a light.

"Cut," 'not again', Jackson felt himself as he began to trembling a little as his new opponent took his stance and began circling cautiously to his right. Jackson naturally responded by moving left. By now cheering voices filled the background reminding him of the high school football games back home. Arms were waving all around him. Everyone in the place had now stood up to watch as the positioning moved in a complete circle. Jackson could see the two guards standing where he had been a few moments ago when he was trying to disappear in fear. Spider had his right hand raised near the guards faces instructing them to "let'm go, let'm fight" . . . they listened.

He threw a punch and so did Jackson. Jackson didn't feel the punch, but he knew it had landed. His left eye exploded into pain as a rainbow of colors swirled around in his head, he was hurt. He responded with a blind punch of his own and once again another boy was decked and trying to get up. Jackson was getting good at this fight game without knowing how.

"Cut"; came the voice of Big Sam. Sam jumped in front of Jackson and immediately began a barrage of hard pinpointed punches. Boom, boom, boom, boom every time he landed a punch Jackson felt as if each of his rib's were snapping against his lungs. Boom, came another blow to Jackson's forehead, sending him hard against the floor. He quickly bounced back up to continue his newly found quest for respect. He was dazed and having trouble keeping his balance. The onlookers began to sound as if they were at a distance and they seemed to spin right along with the room. All the noise momentarily went silent and the facial expressions of those watching seemed to react in slow motion as fatigue wore at Jackson's weary arms. His surprising reign was coming to a quick end as he stumbled into another one of Big Sam's punches. The punches didn't hurt as much as he always thought they would. What was hurting was the fact that he seemed to be losing the fight and he had just learned that he could be a winner. He quickly learned what it felt like to be respected by those he thought he was afraid of.

"Cut"; came the voice of Spider. Spider stepped in, only this time it was Jackson's place that was taken instead of the opponent. 'Thank God' without another word Jackson was out and Spider was in. The expression on Sam's face changed dramatically from confident to doubtful as the two of them squared off. They were standing face to face, fist to fist. Sam threw the same crushing type of blows he had thrown at Jackson. His punches hit nothing. Three light landing blows came from Spider. Sam threw again, this time to the head, again, he hit nothing. Sam's head was jarred back with each jab thrown by Spider. Sam was bleeding and beginning to talk.

"This ain't the Tender Lions fight" he said while throwing three or four lazy jabs to the blocking forearms of Spider. Spider through another barrage of fast punches sounding like the speedy beat of a drum and landing all over Big Sam's body. Sam's arms began to tire; he was a leader, yet he wanted to quit. Spider began to lighten up his punches,

"Anybody wan'na cut on me?" there was no response.

"I wan' a cut on Sam" Jackson said much to his own surprise. Sam looked directly at Jackson and responded,

"No, I'm done, that's it Pittsburgh boy." Just like that Jackson got a nick-name, 'Pittsburgh'.

Spider looked at Jackson and paused for what seemed to be the longest time. "My man" he said, "your my boy, your a Tender Lion, nobody bet-not mess with him" he said loudly while putting his arm around Jackson's neck. Jackson shyly bowed his head though he was feeling mighty proud of his busted lip and swelling eyes. He was still breathing hard but he some how knew he had survived an attack and somehow he had come out on top.

"Let's get ready to bed down". The guard said while slightly smiling after such a show, especially since they didn't have to become involved.

Chapter 4

Jackson's bunk assignment was in the right wing where most of the youths were under age sixteen. With all the excitement going on he had momentarily forgotten about the earlier threatening on-slot from Mohigan. In fact; during all the commotion he was not sure where Mohigan was. Jackson didn't know that Mohigan wasn't, and never had been a gang member. Mohigan had always been institutionalized and that he had never been out in society.

When the lights were turned off a quiet and peaceful silence instantly brought back Jackson's sense of fear and of course, the homesickness. At the foot of his newly assigned bed a bar covered window displayed the starlit night. The beauty of the night indicated that all was right with the world. These were the very same stars and moon that shined through his window back home with one exception. This sky hung over Morganza, and though it held the same beauty, it was lifelessly cold and unfriendly. There was no laughter in the air and as beautiful as it was, it didn't know how to care. The universe just simply sat up above as if it were a still life picture waiting to be exchanged with the morning sun. Where Jackson was born and raised the nights were friendly with the sounds of neighbors talking on their front porches well into the wee hours of each night. Teens would be singing under the streetlights and dogs simply barked at the moon.

Coverdale was a place where you knew all of your neighbors. Where grown-ups often talked about, knowing you since you was born, and reminisced about when your grandparents first came from down south. Jackson never thought he would miss old Mr. 'Hump Back' Jack from just around the corner, Ms. Bee from down the street, who had a small waistline, skinny legs and a very huge butt. Papa Jones, Ms. Lilly or Mr. Grier just to name a few old folks that he didn't know existed when he was back at home among them. He recalled just a few years ago when he played a dirty trick on old Mr. Jack. "Humpback Jack' is the name they called him because he had a huge hump in his back that caused the back of his head to seem lower than the top of his hump. He was so old that it was said that he had once fought in the Mexican war. He was always drunk; in fact, Jackson could not ever remember seeing him sober. His house didn't have an outhouse, so he would walk up the back alley behind Jackson's outhouse to take a leak just beyond the reach of the chain that held Jackson's dog named Nevada. Now . . . Nevada was a huge German shepherd that was too mean for the junkyard that his daddy did business with. They gave him to his dad because no one could go near him without being bitten. Mr. Jack knew exactly how close he could come to Nevada without being bitten. Nevada would get so angry, that he couldn't reach Mr. Jack to bite him, that he would pick up an old rubber tire his dad had given the dog to play with; his mouth was just that big. The dog would bite and shake the tire in frustration. In the mean time, Mr. Jack would take out his ding-a-ling and piss on the dog while mumbling drunken words of torment. One day Jackson, being fed up with Mr. Jack's cruelty to the dog, loosened the stake that held Nevada and move it about two feet closer to where Mr. Jack had come to know as the limits of the dogs chain. Well . . . needless to say, old Mr. Jack staggered up to his favorite pissing spot and commenced his ritual of urinating on the dog. Now Nevada just ran up to the usual limit of his chain and barked, seemingly giving Mr. Jack one more chance to not do his dirty deed. Mr. Jack mumbled and laughed just as he always did and clearly called the dog a worthless hound. Well now, to Mr. Jack's surprise . . . don't you know that Nevada waited for Mr. Jack to finish his pissing and name calling before he leaped and bit Mr. Jack three times, once on the leg, once on the upper thigh and once near the base of his neck. The only thing that saved old Mr. Jack was that the weight of Nevada knocked him out of reach before the dog was done. Of course no one admitted to moving the stake because it was a very dangerous thing to do. Jackson felt bad because Mr. Jack was hurt, he hadn't realized the risk. He just thought that Mr. Jack had it coming.

Those memories of folks like Mr. Jack caused him to miss his two younger sisters Nancy and Colleen and his two younger brothers Chuckie and Rocky even more.

He came from a family of seven, three brothers and three sisters, him being the third born. His stepfather worked in the coal mines of Triadelphia West Virginia. His mother worked on and off in a restaurant someplace, he couldn't remember where; but where ever it was he recollects those foot long hot dogs with mustard that she used to bring home in the middle of the night. They were so good, nothing could compare, not because they tasted that great, but because she brought them home when she was in her best motherly mood. Those hot dogs showed that she cared.

With these warm thoughts, he drifted off to sleep. For the first time since he had arrived in this cottage, he didn't cry, he didn't pray.

Late into the night whispering voices awakened him. A young blond haired boy in the lower bunk next to Jackson's was quietly crying and whimpering, "No, please I don't want to." A white older male was sitting on the edge of his bed stroking his hair and kindly kissing his cheeks as if kissing away his tears.

"You're a pretty thing, um gon'na make sure your all right" he said as he planted another kiss on the cheek of the younger boy while attempting to kiss his lips. The young boy quickly turned his head away and again repeating "please stop, I don't want to."

"If you make me mad I'm gon'na mess you up" he calmly said while tightly squeezing both of the young boys cheeks together between his thumb and for-finger. Looking him in the eyes nose to nose he quickly changed his tone from soft to angry and loud, "you hear me, uh, I said, don't make me f you up?" He began kissing him again this time on the forehead with one hand behind his head and other still squeezing his cheeks.

The young boy shook his head yes, causing him to release his painful grip. The younger boy still quietly sobbed as the older boy lifted himself up and got under the blanket with the younger boy. Jackson wanted to speak up and say, leave him alone, but just as before, he couldn't. He hadn't learned yet how to call on his courage when he needed it. But he had learned how to get angry when someone else was being mistreated.

The whimpering sounds of the younger boy changed as the older boy covered his mouth to prevent him from crying out. Now it was a muffled cry of pain. Jackson couldn't look or listen any longer. The sounds of someone being raped touch his very soul. He squeezed a pillow over his head and attempted to go back to sleep. 'Where is God now', he thought. 'How could he watch this from his thrown? What kind of place is this?' As the night wore on Jackson realized that the same agonizing sounds seemed to be echoing throughout the cottage.

Again Jackson found himself pleading with the heavens and his mother,

"Momma please just get me home." Just before the break of day he finally dozed off again.

Chapter 5

"Rise and shine," came the voice of a guard. "Let's go, get it moving, breakfast in thirty minutes. Make up your bunks, wash-up and line up on the steps.

His first breakfast at cottage five was uneventful, which in it self was a pleasant surprise.

Everyone was assigned to a house duty during the entire stay at the intake cottage. This resulted in an immaculately clean place to live. Jackson's work assignment for the next sixty days was hand washing, waxing and buffing the dining room floor. After each meal, three inmates stacked and remove the chairs and tables from the dining room, which measured about twenty feet by forty feet. With hand held brushes they spent hours on their knees. Each boy aligned at hands reach apart swept from one end of the room to the other. They hand washed the floor with a towels from buckets filled with soap and water. They put pieces of torn blankets on our hands and knees and buffed in a circular motion. As a final touch, they stood up with the blanket pieces on their feet and glided across the room back and forth, side by side, until they could see their reflections in the shiny surface of the hard wood floor below. This process led them to the next meal, following it they started over again. Three times a day every day, they worked the floor to a perfect shine. Doing the dining room floor was considered the best job in the house, considering the options of kitchens, bathrooms, laundry, or the recreation room.

Spider and Squirt were Jackson's work mates. They became as close as one could get in a confined space with such a repetitious daily task. It was a learning experience to work with two well-known Philadelphia killer warlords.

A 'warlord' was as high as you could get before becoming what they called a head, which was sort of a retired gang-banger who no longer had to prove himself as a fighter. They were respected and protected by the gang-bangers and warlords as members who had paid their dues. Spider and Squirt had both taken a liking to Jackson and acknowledge him as their younger brother and an honorary Tender-Lion.

Daily they taught him how to use his hands and eyes to become a defensive street fighter. They believed that one could not survive if you couldn't hold your own on the street. Challenging comrades to fair matches was their way of establishing your rank on the street corners.

A 'corner boy' was a boy from your part of town belonging to the same gang or a gang that had an alliance or treaty. The word 'fair' as in 'fair fight' mentioned earlier was established to prevent and discourage the use of weapons or fights that could result in death.

It was understood that; too often there were cowards who would occasionally take the life of another gang member as an act of revenge caused by disrespect or embarrassment. Most shootings and stabbing were generally crimes committed by young cowards or older people in their late twenties in disputes over things like women or drugs. These dumb reasons for violence were not welcome in the street laws of young gangs. In the gangs it was all about pride courage and fellowship.

Most of the time between the cleaning task, they spent boxing with light punches to body and an occasional slip to the head would cause a little blood, but generally it was not intended.

Jackson had introduced a custom from his home corner. Since the folks of his community never tolerated fighting, it was singing that took center stage instead of boxing. Singing was a primary way to establish popularity in Coverdale, and though young, he knew most of the lyrics to the popular and the old songs that his brother used to sing back home.

His older brother Larry was an avid fan of spiritual groups like the Swan Silvertones, Blind Boys, Caravans, Soul Stirrers, to name a few. He would occasionally hit a note from the soul groups that were known as crooners, like the Drifters, Dells, Spaniels or the Del-vikings.

On his streets, singing groups would form and compete by singing and adding showmanship. Bragging rights around Pittsburgh was for the community with the best group. Talent shows and singing contest were the call. The benefits were girls, popularity, and sometimes money.

Spider and Squirt liked the idea of singing in harmony and looked forward to being drilled by the young Jackson to learn the words to songs and hitting the right notes, instead of each other.

At one point, they had gotten so good gliding back and forth over the shiny dining room floor singing "Walk With the Wind", that one of the guards asked if they would perform for guest on, special visitors' day. The guards believed that it may be a way to ease some of the fear parents had about the rough and terrible stories that were being told.

They were assigned two more boys to the dining room floor detail, so they could practice with the customary five-person group. Later, when they were assigned to a permanent cottage, the five went to cottage six, where they could croon and entertain for the entire prison on special occasions.

A lot of the violence began to subside as more and more groups began to form in other cottages. Jackson's new job in cottage six was to organize talent shows and decorate staging for what was becoming a once a month activity.

The battle of the groups became the pride of each cottage. The fights were still occurring, the rapes were still a part of life, but the overall violent atmosphere was slowly toning down. Jackson felt special and so did most of the youth involved. They now looked forward to someday going home with a new talent and stories other than survival tales.

Chapter 6

Six months later;

    Spider, warlord of the Tender Lions and Squirt, warlord of the Vikings and a Pittsburgh boy, had set the tempo for cottage six. Real fighting became rare. Harmony was not only in the music it had begun to spread to the everyday attitude. Youths began requesting to be transferred to cottage six to get away from the daily threats or violence and rape. The character of each cottage seemed to be determined by the youths that were in control. To the guards, it was just a job, no reason to risk life or limb trying to control fifty or sixty boys with their minds set on disrupting each others lives.

    The population of cottage six stayed at its maximum. Boys went home faster due to good behavior. They introduce other arts like oil painting and dance showmanship.

    The guards of other cottages began to use cottage six as a reward for those who stayed on good behavior. The waiting list and request for cottage six lengthen. Incoming younger boys were listed to go to cottage six upon their entry into the intake cottage, to avoid the rapes that previously had become common place.

    The dormitory type sleeping quarters were replaced by cubicles that were locked down at night to make rapes more difficult. A change had come. Perhaps some prayers were answered. Jackson was destined to be an imperative part of the change. He was young, gifted and now learning to be a proud comrade. His compassion and protective instincts overcame his youthful lack of courage. This was now his cottage. They lived and got along like people in Coverdale, not Philadelphia, Pittsburgh or any other inner city.

Chapter 7

When new boys were assigned to cottage six, they were immediately welcomed to a sense unexpected safety that had never existed before. Cottage six had special privileges like extra movies, easier jobs and most importantly, no contact with cottages one two or three, which were still hardcore cottages set aside for trouble makers and older youths that had been sentenced for violent crimes.

Morganza had a theater of its own that was also used as a stage for music and other positive activities. The line up for theater was a Saturday morning spectacle. Each cottage assembled its youth on the eight-foot walkway that led into the theater. Just as they did on the night of the 'big escape' previously mentioned. Movie day and time was moved to 10:00 a.m. Saturdays to prevent the temptation of running away. Runaways still occurred as they always had but seldom did anyone escape and when they attempted they were often brought back and sent to Cottage one or sent to White Hill as punishment.

Any line up for any event had to follow the rules of Morganza and more importantly the rules of the streets of Philly. Leaders were always positioned at the front of their groups. This was generally established by boxing matches or just recognition that one boy or another was a warlord on the street and unchallenged at his position. The cottage six line-up went like this; front left Spider, to his right Squirt, Big Sam and Sholtz, all warlords of the most power gangs of Philly and recognized for their reputation as street fighters by all of the other cottage inmates, including the ruffians of cottages one, two and three. And yet, they were all residents of, what now was labeled the good cottage.

Lined in front of six was Cottage three, lead by a boy name Mouse, followed by Little John, Mohigan and Tank all, notorious fighters and known rapist.

At the tail end of each group, were the smaller, weaker boys often, considered girls by bullies such as Mohigan.

Jackson's position behind Spider was considered one of the most important and wanted positions of a gang leader. To line behind a warlord, even though Jackson was not really a Tender Lion, was an honor. Spider chose Jackson as his backup. Truth was, his skills in boxing had developed quickly. He could hold his own with any of the feared warlords. Rumor had it that Jackson was now the second hardest puncher at Morganza, second only to Russell Sholtz. Jackson had swiftly grown to nearly six foot two and was weighing about two hundred fifteen pounds. He had just turned fourteen. He was seldom challenged to a boxing match. Those ahead of him couldn't risk the chance of being beaten by a Pittsburgher, so they left that possibility alone by making him one of them.

When they arrived at the theater girls from the girls' section were already seated well out of reach in the right section of the theater. The boys entered based on their ranking. Warlords of each cottage were always last to enter. Spider and Squirt, though from the weakest cottage, they were known throughout Morganza and at home in Philly as the two most notorious fighters of their time.

Once everyone in Morganza had been seated there was always a pause and then the entering of the killer warlords from cottage six. First, Big Sam, then Squirt and last with whistle and applauds of a super star came Spider himself. He strolled in with a hard looking gangster face. He dressed in Philly stile street cloths just like some of the others but he wore his differently. He strolled like a warlord that ruled every thing around him. One could feel it in the air. All of the boys yearned to be like him, to look like him with his tall lean body structure, his processed straight black hair. He knew just how to profile for the girl's section. At one point it seemed that every female in building was instantly filled with desire. To see him walk in was the treat of the week. Jackson watched and wished. He didn't want to get all of the attention that the young handsome warlord was getting. All he wanted was to be respected by the gang-bangers that were being so admired. He wanted that kind of power. He wanted to instill that kind of fear in the bullies. And, he wanted that kind comradeship with those that had the roars of lions and compassion of a mother for her child. He observed every move, every slight turn of the face, every motion that indicated that proud dominating self-respect. Yes, this one young boy was a marvel for any one that looked his way and that happened to be everyone in the place. No one could ever grow tired of this weekly moment of excitement.

More and more each week the girls began to recognize Jackson. He had learned to stroll swinging one arm and holding his nuts with the other, just like Spider. He too wore his pants high water style with suspenders pulling them up just under his breast muscles. This was his way of imitating the warlords and their show of dominance. It had gotten to a point that other cottage warlords became irritated by the fact that a Pittsburgh boy was being recognized by the girls more than some of them. Warlords from other cottages gave gestures and challenging signs as a show of contempt only to find Spider, Squirt and Big Sam making them back off and sit. It was as if getting to Jackson meant coming through them and no one was up to that much of a challenge.

One day Jackson was sent to Cottage #3 to pick up a five gallon container of milk that was left on their dock, supposedly by mistake. Jackson knew that this was not a good thing. He felt a little of his previous fears coming back along with the aspect of entering Cottage #3. This venture was equal to going into another gang's territory without permission, again, not a good thing. Later he discovered that a guard who thought he, meaning Jackson, needed a little lesson and had set him up.

Alone, he entered onto the dock of cottage #3. The waiting guard instructed him to go to the recreation room and wait until the container was filled; again this was not a good thing. As he entered their domain a hush fell upon the room. They couldn't believe their eyes. Here was the young, cocky, well liked Pittsburgh boy in the mist of the enemies that would like nothing better than to notch their belt by giving Jackson a real good old-fashion Philly ass whoop'n.

"Pittsburgh . . . how you fill without Spider on yo hip?" the voice was that of Mouse the head banger of Cottage #3. To his side was Jackson's most feared adversary, none other than Mohigan. Four or five others had started gathering around. Jackson recognized a Tender Lion and gave the gang sign for support.

"That shit ain't work'n here. Cottage #3 is run by The Valley, not the Tender Lions," Mouse quickly said in effort to stop any support Jackson might try and get from his adopted gang members.

"We're gon'na kick yo ass real good pretty boy" this comment coming from the number one rapist Mohigan.

"Then um gon'na f ya and make ya my girl, 'Mr. Pittsburgh', just like I wanted to do over in cottage five," he said.

Jackson's courage was failing him more by the minute. He could feel fear taking over, seemingly inch by inch. Jackson was doing all that he could to keep his hands from trembling. The familiar sound of his pounding heart amplified as loud as it ever had in the past. He began breathing hard and uncontrollably while moving and putting his back against the wall.

"Gim'me a fair" he asked looking at Mouse.

"No-no fair" Mohigan responded.

"Your git'n yo ass kicked royally, you came on our turf with yo sissy ass." The intensity was building quickly. Another second brought this group of about eight hostile gang-bangers directly in front of Jackson. Spider had taught him that if anyone stepped within arms reach without a fair being called, to fire your best shot at whoever was nearest to your right.

Jackson felt his instinctive courage returning just as quickly as it had left. On his right was Mohigan. Jackson hated him and all that he stood for. This was going to be the punch for all the young boys Mohigan had raped, and for all the boys who he had painstakingly made their lives a big regretful secret. Jackson gave the Tender Lion's gang sign once more hoping to get some back up.

"Um down with him" came the voice of a Tender Lion. He was a small stocky built boy by the name of Two, Two slid in beside him with his hands raised.

"Hold up" said Mouse "this ain't bout to lead to war between the Lions and the Valley, let's go wit'ta fair."

"Who you want?" he asked Jackson. Without hesitation Jackson boldly pointed and said, "Mohigan." Before he could pull his hand back, Mohigan struck a blow to the left side of his face while at the same time pushing his whole body against Jackson in an effort to knock him off his feet. His weight caught Jackson off balance, causing him to slam hard against the block wall behind him. Mohigan followed with another blow that struck Jackson's neck and then a third blow that struck him in the eye. Jackson could only see a mixture of floating colors from his left eye. He had yet to throw a punch and already he felt beaten and confused. Mohigan paused and stepped back into a fight posture knowing he had hurt Jackson.

"I toll-you didn't I. I toll-you I was gon'na kick yo ass". Jackson was blinking his eyes trying to refocus and get into the fight.

"Cut," said the Tender Lion on Jackson's behalf.

"No," Jackson responded "no cut." Mohigan struck Jackson instantly in the mouth. Causing him stagger and sway as if he were ready to drop. He curled his body downward in pain and took a few more punches without responding with his own. Mohigan kept right-on taunting and punched every where he spotted a place to land his fist.

"Come on bitch do some'thin. I toll-you did'n I". The upper-half of Jackson's body was tucked way down into a crouching position when he finally managed to strike his first blow to Mohigan's stomach. It landed dead center just below the middle of his ribs. The single punch sounded like a baseball hitting a catchers-mit. He followed instinctively with another. It landed in the same spot. Mohigan responded to each blow with the sound of someone throwing up bad food. Jackson, surprising even himself, stood upright and instantly threw a right hook, catching him on his way down in response to the belly shots. The force of Jackson's punch tore the flesh of Mohigan's left cheek exposing his mouth filled with blood. Mohigan tumbled to the floor. In an instant his eyes were jerking up into his head while he still attempted to get back onto his feet . . . with no luck.

"Damn!" someone said, in response to the cracking noise from the punch that had finally reached Jackson's ears. Mohigan's teeth on the left side of his face were in full view. Blood and saliva was pouring from the open gash. Everyone looked stunned, including Jackson. The tide had turned quickly and the fear had made its leap to everyone nearby including "Two" who had stepped in to help Jackson.

"Come on Mouse it's your turn," Jackson gestured with his hands raised in the boxing position, "you can be next." Now it was Jackson's turn to fester for a fight. Without a response from Mouse, he threw two hard blows to his chest as he spoke. Jackson saw in his eyes that he was also in shock due to the sight of Mohigan who was lying on the floor jerking his legs as if going into convulsions.

"Null man, we just wanted to see if you had heart, your all right wit us." This was a pleading voice, pleading but trying to keep a slight image for his stable.

"Let's call it done man." Mouse said. Jackson, with a pumped up heart, looked around the room imitating the look of the proud warlords that he had come to know in his own cottage after a victory.

"Anybody else want me?" There were no takers. He was the man. Pounding on his own chest with both fists while still standing over Mohigan, Jackson roared, "Get up you ain't hurt!" With a soft kick to Mohigan's mid-section he walked out onto the dock where he took the milk from a stunned young guard and headed back to his cottage.

Within a week, word about the fight between Jackson and the Valley gang of cottage three had spread all over Morganza. The following Saturday at the theater Spider stopped Jackson from entering in his usual position. He whispered, "your last today Pittsburgh." He gave Jackson the gang sign and told Sam, Squirt and Shaults to entered before him. The girls gave up the usual acknowledgment to the killer warlords. Spider remarked just before he left Jackson outside, "just this once I'm step'n aside, you earned it. Don't let it go to your head." Before Jackson could refuse the often wished for honor, Spider turned and stepped inside. Outside of the theater door Jackson nervously paused for what seemed to be the longest time. Everyone in the place was waiting for him to enter. He wanted to bust in like a gang leader but instead of feeling cocky and awesome, he felt shy and out of place. As he slowly entered he looked into the eyes of his comrades who had formed an isle for his entry. Both Spider and Squirt gave their perspective gang victory signs. The girls screamed and applauded. Even the guards began to slowly clap. To avoid dropping some heart felt tears of pride, Jackson reached and held up Spider's left hand and Squirt's right as if they were a team. He made one fast move and strolled out in front of both of them in his rightful place. He didn't want to be recognized as thee warlord. He wanted to be known as the nice kid that's always in trouble, just like he was back home. He could feel his stomach drawing itself inwards and bringing on the emotions that have often caused him to feel strangely weak inside. In his own mind he had concluded that when he felt this way his tears were falling inside and dropping upon his heart. This was his way of being tough. This way no one would ever see him cry because he's happy about something. He had to be strong . . . and proud . . . and fearless.

"Today I thank the man upstairs that I'm someone special among my own," he said to himself.

The monthly visits from home never failed. Jackson's mother came every month like clockwork. He told her stories about Morganza, she told him stories of what was happening back home. Things never change in Coverdale. Things at Morganza never stayed the same. Living in peace, we began serving time and making the best of what we had. Work was a five-day event, Movies on Saturday and rest on Sunday. The evenings were filled with practice singing sessions. At night they were still bedded down by nine P.M. The nights never stopped being tearful and long, though the cry for God's help did diminished. The acceptance of not going home had long sat in. A few weeks later one of the guards that had learned to respect Jackson for handling the cottage #3 incident, decided to give Jackson a special treat. He sent Jackson down to the dairy docks with one of the weekly orders for the cottage breakfast milk. This was an assignment that only the guards performed, mainly because it was the one place that the female prisoners worked with limited supervision and it was off limits to any male prisoners. None the less Jackson was given the one hour weekly trek that took him amidst the young girls of Morganza. On the first day he arrived, the dock supervisor instructed him to wait out on dock steps until his order was handled. Jackson took his place at the top of the steps and sat there alone waiting for the next instruction. He listened as the young girls inside of the building were talking and laughing as if they were as happy as a lark. This was as close as he had come to a female since he arrived at the institution. The tones of their voices caused a feeling of warmth inside that made him feel a certain desire he had only dreamed of. After glancing around to see if anyone was watching him, he stood up and slowly walked over to an open doorway in the direction of the female voices. Inside there were twelve or so young girls working, most of them were facing away from him. Remaining in the shadows and out of their sight, he found himself staring. 'They were all beautiful; they were girls, wow girls.' He looked from one to another, adoring each and every one of them. From head to toe, he glanced again and again, to a point that began feeling a little guilty that he may be violating them in some way. They continued to talk and giggle and he continued to be mesmerized by their mere presence. After a few moments his eyes locked in on one of the girls. As pretty as they all were, this one stood out in his mind. After all the gawking she suddenly took all of his attention. She was a little taller than average. She was brown skinned with an unusually long neck, and legs that seemed to never end. She was relatively thin with a flawless complexion that was complimented by her small but perfectly round breast. Her eyes were very dark brown surrounded by the pure white of innocence. She was seemingly shy. Even though she laughed at everything being said, she slightly blushed each time the laughter faded. While he was looking into her eyes from afar, she glanced over towards him and quenched her eyes as if she may have seen him. He dodge backwards further out of sight as they continued to talk as if they didn't have a problem in the world. Jackson was about to peak back around the corner when an unseen girl standing behind him ask, "what are you doing here?" She said it loud enough that all the girls inside heard and came out onto the dock to see who she were talking to. "Look what I found here" she said to the others as they gathered closer. "Hey" Jackson said in an awkward greeting. One of the girls remarked "I've seen you before; your from cottage six with Spider and his corner boys."

By now he was completely surrounded by the group of girls. The one he was so attracted to standing just to his left and looking him right in the face. One of the girls, seemingly the most outspoken, asked "what's your name "Jackson, but they call me Pittsburgh," he answered. Another asked "where you from?" And another asked, "how'd you get here?" Question after question without a pause for an answer until the one that first found him stopped every thing by saying,

"I found him, he's mine."

"Wait a minute," said the out spoken one who now seemed to be the leader

"He's too young for you and he's too cute for all of us" They all broke out in laughter.

"How'd you get here cutie . . . oh, I mean Pittsburgh," she said in a mocking way and getting another burst of laughter from the group. "I brought the milk order for cottage six."

"How old are you?"

"I'm sixteen" Jackson answered with a bold faced lie.

"Well I'll tell ya, if you were a little older you'd be mine. You like girls?"

"Yea."

One of the other girls grabbed his hand playfully and claimed,

"Okay, I'll take'm, he's mine." This cute claim brought another burst of laughter as they all began to circle and look him up and down. Jackson had not really experience any intimacy, though he had played around with girls back home with touchy feely type love acts, but never the true act of love making and the girls seem to sense that he was shy and countrified.

"Which one of us do-ya like Jack?" Jackson hunched his shoulders proving he was as they thought; a little country boy who was just big for his age.

"Come on pick one of us for a kiss before they make us go back to work."

"I'll kiss'm," said one of the girls.

"No, let him pick somebody and the rest of us will walk away. Come on cute Jackson, Pittsburgh or what ever your name is, pick one of us, we won't bite you." Jackson didn't know what to do or say. He knew which one he wanted but he was much to shy to say anything. He kept shyly rolling his eyes, but each time he looked around he ended up looking into the brown eyes of the one girl that was making his heart strangely throb.

"You want Jean? Is that why you keep looking at her like she some sort of angel, is that who you want?"

"I don't know" Jackson answered. Everyone laugh again, except Jean, who like Jackson, stood looking honored but dumbfounded.

"Wow, talking about a match, these two deserve each other they're both country," said the outspoken one. "Let's leave them alone girls, who knows, they may speak to each or something." With that being said, they file away one at a time from Jackson, leaving him out on in the shadows of the dock alone with Jean. Jackson's heart was throbbing at a pace he didn't think possible. It was pounding so loud he thought she would hear, it and laugh again like before. Instead, she just smiled at him, exhaled . . . and lowered her head. His mind was racing, trying to think of what to say

"Hi," he blurted out, kind of stupidly.

"Hi," she said in return, without lifting her head. What would Spider do if he were in this predicament? He wondered.

"Your name is Jean," he seemed to be telling her instead of asking or confirming.

"I know," she answered, with a slight chuckle, after realizing how silly her response was. They were both looking everywhere but at each other. Someone in the work area spoke loudly saying,

"Good God, touch her or kiss her or something before I go crazy in here." There was another burst of laughter from inside the room where everyone was apparently being quite enough to hear what was being said out on the dock.

"Let's walk out on the lot where they can't be so nosy," she said. She instinctively grabbed his hand and pulled him along side of her. Jackson didn't hesitate, he happily went along smiling and trying not to look so awkward. Within a minute they were alone and back to the awkward feelings that would not go away. The difference was that, they were still holding each others hand and they were in no way going to let go. The feeling that came with just holding her hand was more intimate than any love making that he could imagine. Neither of them spoke a word for at least five minutes. They just stood there being shy, until Jean ask, "you like me?" That was easy for Jackson to answer

"Yes," he answered while shaking his head, "a lot".

"I like you too. Even though we just met, I feel like I've known you forever. I don't know why". She reached over and grabbed Jackson's other hand and stood facing him. "I've never had a boy friend. My parents were killed in an auto accident when I was eleven. They couldn't find a foster home for me, so I've been here since I turned twelve three years ago. Why are you here?"

"I got into trouble with the police and they sent me here as punishment."

"What did you do?"

"I was bad, I was fighting all the time with bullies." he lied. Jackson reasoned that it was more impressive to be a fighter than a thief. This was the first time he realized that being a thief was embarrassing and that fighting was worthy of pride. After another long pause she asked Jackson.

"Do you really want to be my boy friend?"

"Yea" Jackson responded.

"Why," she asked.

"Cause your pretty and you seem nice."

One of the other girls interrupted and told Jean she had to come back in, they were getting ready to go back to their cottage. Jean quickly moved up closer to Jackson, and before he knew it, she put her lips against his and kissed him. He felt the weight of her upper body in his arms as her knees momentarily buckled and he in-return, kissed her back. After a few seconds she pulled away weakened and slightly panting.

"I've got to go. I hope we see each other again soon." She hurriedly said

"I like you a lot Jackson. I don't know why or how, but I do." As she walked away, Jackson said, "I like you too, and I'll see you again no matter what it takes." In few seconds she was inside and the door was slammed shut.

His milk order was sitting on the steps waiting for him. In no time, Jackson was walking back to cottage six. He felt like a new boy. He was walking so fast and grinning so hard, that he began to sing one of the songs he sang back home when he was happy . . . *"Walking along . . . my merry way . . . Singing a song . . . oh happy day . . . Singing a song . . . I'm just walking along . . . When I'm walking I feel like a king, when I'm singing, I don't care bout a thing, When I'm feel'n, the way I do, you love me, oh and I love you . . . walking along"*

Jackson returned to the docks once a week for five weeks yearning and desperately looking for Jean. He could not get her off of his mind. He was beginning to doubt his ability to keep his word to her about seeing her again no matter what. He sent several notes to her cottage hoping she would respond, but nothing came back. The girls that he did see at the docks were different girls than those who were with Jean. They began to get friendlier and flirtier each week, but all he would do is ask them to give word to Jean that he misses her and that he has been looking for her every week. Two months went by and he began to realize that he probably would never see her again. His resistance to the other girls on the docks had diminished to a point that he wanted to move on and find out what it would be like to hold some one else's hand. Then one day one of the girls from the original group, informed him that Jean, while yearning for Jackson, became vulnerable and had fallen under the spell of one of the bigger girls in her cottage. Jackson was broken hearted and sickly in love with the brown beauty and vowed that he would win her back some how. In the mean time he had to go on with his young and inexperienced life.

Chapter 8

A Story: 'The Speakeasy'

One night after the lights had gone off Jackson was asked why he was here. He didn't seem to belong. The answer was a short story that was the first of many. It sometimes became so quiet while Jackson told his stories that he often thought all his listeners had fallen asleep, but when he paused he would hear their confirming questions from all over the wing, "then what happened?"

"I'll tell you how I got here but first let me tell you about my life back in Coverdale." He started with a story of how and why he knew the lyrics of so many songs.

"When I was about eight years old my father added three small bedrooms and an indoor bathroom to our two bedroom house. Before that, we and most of the other families in Coverdale, had what we called an 'outhouse'; which was an outside bathroom located about thirty feet behind each of the A framed houses that everyone lived in. My dad was one of the first to bring the toilet into the house with inside running water. Anyway . . . my mother, being a natural hustler, whether it be collecting numbers or selling pop and candy, decided it would be a good idea to open a speakeasy on the bottom floor of the two floor addition. It started out as a little event but after a few weeks word had spread that it was one of the jumpiness places outside of Pittsburgh. People were coming from miles around to play the jukebox and dance to the be-bop music well up and into the wee hours of the morning. Me and my younger brother and sister slept in the rooms right above the dance floor and most of the nights while the music was playing we were wide awoke listening and singing to the beat of the late night jams. Even when there was nothing going on down stairs we would lie awake and play a game we called 'see who can name a song the fastest'. The idea was to start humming or sing a few beats of a song and who ever named that song first was the winner and had the right to start singing the next song. That's how I learn the words to so many songs that I should be too young to remember.

But here's the good part . . . we had pried a crack in the floor of my room so we could look down through the crack and watch the older people dance. One Saturday night I was all alone and looking through the crack at a lady that had come out from the city. Before she came in I had looked out my window and seen her coming. She was so fine, and while she was walking in, someone played a song on the jukebox called 'So Fine'. It seemed to be right on-time. I scrambled to my peeking crack and watched her as she switched her hips and snapped her fingers on the way through the door. She was smiling at everyone as she moved her shoulders to the beat. The crowd was edging her on. 'Ah get it girl,' someone said. 'Shake that thang baby. Come on baby show us what you got.' She moved to center of the floor and pulled her dress right up and tucked it between her legs. She was ready. She started dancing like nobody I had seen before. Her legs were prettier than any legs in the world. She had spiked heels and dark stockings with a heavy black line sewn up the back. Her blouse was so low cut that you could see the space between her breasts. And, from above where I was peeking, I swear to you, when she moved a certain way I could see the dark part of her tits. As the first song ended another began, it was a song called, 'Work with me Annie'. She paused for a second, wiggled a little bit and then said, "a-h-h shit they done played my song." Then she really got down. She pulled up her dress even higher than before, this time exposing her girder belts at the very top of her stockings. I was going crazy. I wanted to call out to Chuckie to come see this woman dance but I was so mesmerized that I had to stay there with my eye so tight against the crack that when I did pull back I had the imprint of the floor crack from my forehead to my chin. At first she was dancing by her self while everybody, both men and women, stood around her and clapped. They played the song again but she had never stopped moving her body to the music. And then, from out of the crowd, a short thin guy with a broad grin and a gold tooth sparkling in the lights, apparently couldn't take it any more. He jump out onto the floor in front of her, did a little spin and then a leaping split. He started his own dance right between her legs. 'Go head Joe show her what a country boy can do. Go boy go. Burn her man, burn her good.'

With that encouragement Joe went to work. It was a hot night and the sweat of the man was running down his face as he grinded against her body to the beat. I don't know if he was hot from heat of the night or the excitement of the dance. I just know I was on fire. They kept right on grinding to the rhythm of the beat while everyone in the room was cheering them on and trying to get her to lift her dress even higher. The woman flung her jet black hair wig back off of face like white women do; she was ready. She was looking right into his eyes while moving her shoulders and swaying her hips from side to side and smiling all the while. She snapped her fingers so loud that I could hear them up through the crack and then she gestured for him to 'bring it on' with her forefinger. She began to bend over backwards with her knees wide apart as if she was doing the limbo. As her head went all the way back I would swear to you that she looked up and winked right at me. Her lips were wet and juicy and painted heavily with dark red lipstick that looked like honey. Her eyelashes surrounded by blue mascara seemed to curl over and touch cheeks and eye brows. I watched and panted with pleasure until I nearly fainted. The guy Joe was doing his best to burn her but she was just too good. He got bold enough to reach his hands around her and pull her body forward against him with his face nearly touching hers. Me . . . I was still glued to the crack like you wouldn't believe. The crowd was clapping louder and louder. They were humping each other harder and harder. The music and the laughter from the crowd was so driving that I thought I was going to explode with excitement. Her smile turned to a serious look of passion as she stepped forward nudging the man with the lower part of her stomach. The man lost control and tried to kiss her but she put her hand on his face just in time to push him away while continuing her dance. She slowly danced back down to the floor and on her way back upright she pushed him away from her again as if his hands had finally gone too far. The show was over . . . The crowd clapped and whistled for a job well done. Everybody started to move to the center of the floor and do their own dance. The party was about to start but it was over for me. I was too exhausted to watch anymore. I remember going off to sleep with a smile from ear to ear and thinking I had slightly wet my pants. I don't recall ever seeing such a woman as that one again. I'll never forget her face and how she looked at me while she captivated everybody there. I don't care what anybody says, I know she seen me and she winked right at me. I'm still captivated to this day."

Jackson's told stories like these one after another and everyone listened, including the guards. He had come from a family of story tellers from his African and Indian ancestors. The stories just kept on coming.

A Story 'The purse caper'

"Let me tell you a story that I believe was one of my best adventures as a kid. Once when I was only about ten, we did what we called our 'purse caper'. By then I was considered a bad ass little boy, though I didn't really know I was bad at all. One Friday night three friends and I had walked to the high school to watch a football game. The entry tickets were selling for sixty cents each. I had only a nickel. My friends Pootie, Donnie and Greg threw in with about eighteen cents. We were still a long way from getting through the front gates. I notice that there were two separate entry gates. It didn't take much to realize that if we could get one ticket we could pass it through the fence until we were all inside. But still we had only twenty-three cents between us, which was not enough to get even one of us in. We needed to beg some money and we could only accomplished that with Donnie's help. He was the smallest of all of us and he had blond hair and blue eyes. When he put on his most pathetic face and pleaded with each person that passed by for a nickel, no sympathetic women could refuse. After eight heart softening pleas we had enough for our ticket with change to spare.

It's very hard for an opportunistic youth to keep his face pressed against the glass without his mind working out a way to get where the action was. Logic says to use whatever means necessary to be a part of those who were eating, drinking and being merry as opposed to stress and failure at age ten.

On the hillsides above the football field, there were twenty or so black faces against the wire fence cheering for the two black boys from Coverdale. Most were teenagers; a few were family members just watching the excitement of a young senior nicknamed 'Toes' carry the ball. I wanted to hand them our ticket stub so they could get in just as we did but knowing if I did they would say, 'Jackie that's wrong, um gon'na tell your momma'. 'Jackie' was a nickname I was sometimes called by folks that knew me as a kid. Coverdale is a Baptist community. If the Bible said it, then that's the way it had to be. On the other hand, Coverdale had three speak-easy's, several numbers runners and an occasional sex scandal, usually one or two guys making their rounds with any female who may have lowered her resistance. But to this day most people there don't lock their doors or take the keys out of their car.

My second level of this crime-spree was figuring out how to get other friends from Coverdale into the game. One Friday night, a ticket taker realized that no black boy had bought a ticket and asked me how I got in. He summoned me to come to him but instead, I just broke out running with him right on my tail trying to catch me. I didn't have a stub so I decided to run and lose him in the crowd. He would have had a better chance at catching Toes. I zig-zagged through the crowd like Jim Brown, occasionally running backwards so he could catch up. I taunted him 'catch me if you can'. White men shouted 'catch that little nigger'. By now everyone in the stadium was cheering for me as I made move after move avoiding the security. I even ran out onto the edge of the football momentarily disrupting the game. From out of nowhere a bystander grabbed me saying 'I got him, I got the little nigger boy.' I kicked and squirmed trying to get him off of me. At the time I couldn't figure out why this big white man grabbed me. This wasn't fair; he wasn't a part of the chase. He had lifted me completely off the ground but I didn't give up, I continued to kick and holler. A white lady standing near bye said to the man 'you leave that boy alone.' She came to my aid pulling at him as if I was her own child. She caused enough concern to make the man loosen his grip for a second and I was back onto my feet and running again like a bat out of hell. Pootie, Donnie and Greg came from out of nowhere and they were running along side of me as we headed for cover. We ran and turned under the bleachers; safe at last. We sat there thinking we were out of harms way. We began to watch the game and talk and laugh about my close encounter when all of a sudden the crowd stood to its feet and there was thunking sound of something hitting the ground right next to me. Someone's purse had fallen through the bleachers and right to us. I immediately grabbed it and ran a few steps away from the area. When I looked inside my eyes nearly jumped from their socket. There was money inside, big money. We danced around like it was Christmas. There was at least four dollars in change. We weren't interested in the paper money, which at the time we thought only adults could spend. But the coins . . . wow this was it. By now a man had stuck his head through the bleachers looking for the pocket-book. I ran over and handed it to him. He said thank you as we moved to the rear thinking of how we were going to spend our loot. Hot dogs and pop was a unanimous decision. I loved hot dogs. They were 15 cents and pop was a dime. Pootie was white, so he was sent out to buy them for us. We ate, drank and talked of our adventure. I could not help but notice the pocket-books sitting near almost every white woman on the bleachers. All those dangling and inviting straps hanging everywhere we looked. We're gon'na be rich, I thought. One after another we removed the coins from each and every purse. I was going to give my mom a million dollars so she wouldn't have to work. I couldn't wait 'til next Friday night's game to make some more money. For the rest of the football season we paid our own way in and went right to work under the bleachers. We had more money than any one of us knew could possibly exist."

From out of nowhere came the voice of a security guard, "good story Pittsburgh. Let's try and get some sleep though huh guys." This voice was unusually kind. The bedtime praying and crying was pretty much a thing of the past. Morganza was truly becoming home.

A Story 'The police rob Sears'

"Here's another true story I think you will like. One warm September night my comrades Eddie Brooks, Billy Muldoon, an older man named Bobby and myself jointly decided that we would break into Sears. This is the caper that ultimately caused me to end up here. After two years of breaking into stores and businesses and no longer able to make the claim that they were innocent pranks for coins, I had become the local boy who could convince even young adults that we could take from those who have plenty without harming anyone and without a chance of being caught. I guess in reality we all had pretended that what we were doing was more of an act of Robin Hood than an act of any kind of crime. In fact I'm not sure that I knew exactly what a crime was. All I really wanted to do was have enough money to be admired by my friends and to help out with the things my daddy was working around the clock to get for our household. The crime tools were a sledgehammer, a pry bar, a metal punch and three flashlights that I borrowed from my daddy's tool shed. The oldest of the group and the only adult among us, had an old pick up truck. He parked about three hundred yards from the Sears driveway. His job was to warn us if anyone drove onto the lot by turning on his lights. And of course to drive us there and back home once we were done doing our devilment. When we reached our designated pickup point, Billy Muldoon's job was stand at the rear of the building to warn us if Bobby's flashed his lights. Eddie and I got inside by punching a hole in the side of the cement block building with the sledgehammer where there were no alarms. There were no houses nearby, so there was no way anyone would hear the pounding. We always punched the holes away from the doors or windows. We learned long ago that if the police came they would come through the doors or windows while we escape from the block hole. Our goal was to find and take cash and small appliances that could be sold to the local magistrate who was operating a fence. A fence is a person that buys and sells stolen goods. We had entered Sears for no more than fifteen minutes when Billy's warning light was shined into the rear window. Moving quickly we ran to our newly made exit and climbed through. We crossed the asphalt parking lot and up onto a hillside over looking the rear door. A police car pulled into the lot and then another pulled in beside him. We could see Bobby start his truck, make a u-turn and speed off, leaving us stranded on the hillside. There were three police men shining lights into the building one motioned to the other two to come and look through the windows where we had apparently stacked a box of cameras we'd located before exiting. They looked for a place of entry but did not see the hole that was out of view and behind a trash bin. They talked for a few moments. They suddenly leaned back and kicked in the back door. With guns drawn they entered the building. After what seemed like an eternity, one of the officers came out carrying the cameras and put them into the trunk of the police cruiser. He re-entered again and came out carrying a few small appliances. After several such trips he filled both vehicles with merchandise. A little later a truck pulled up into the lot and drove to the rear dock. The door was opened from the inside and now five men were hastily loading the truck with goods. All but one of the vehicles drove off leaving the one officer alone. He turned on his flashing lights and appeared to be waiting. We had no choice but to stay out of sight and wait for him to leave, knowing we'd be spotted if we tried to exit the enclosed fenced area. Another car pulled into the lot. We had made ourselves comfortable looking out from the brush hoping they'd leave and we could begin our trek back to Coverdale empty handed. After a long discussion with who seemed to be an owner, the police officer left leaving the latest arrival alone. He immediately began to load his vehicle with bags and articles from the store into the trunk of his car. Feeling safe we then ventured out of hiding and walked along the side a ten feet fence until we reach an opening to the street. Ducking every car, we made it home, physically worn out from this night's strange caper. The following day the news reported a major burglary believed to have been committed by a so called burglary ring that had been active over the last year. Thousands of dollars in cash and goods were reported taken. About three months later we were arrested for the crime."

"Wow, you got'ta be kid'n me, they took all the loot and you guys took the fall."

"Yeah, charged as juveniles there was no trial just a police officer making his case and a judge to do the sentencing and, after all . . . we were actually guilty. Good night guys."

The next morning Jackson headed for the dairy dock on his weekly trek. He had pretty much accepted that, he had seen the last of Jean though she was constantly on his mind. As he topped the steps a young girl inside the work area motion for him to wait. She walked up to him and handed him a note. He slowly walked a few steps while unfolding the piece of paper thinking that he may have a new secret pen pal. The note read 'Meet me out behind the dairy at the storage tanks.' *Jean.*

Jackson's heart came to a screeching halt. He found himself nearly running off the dock and down around the building without question and certainly without hesitation. When he came to what he assumed were the storage tanks, he slowed down and began to calmly look for her. She was no where to be found, it reminded him of a time when he was younger, when one Christmas morning he had ran down his steps and found that the bike that he thought he was getting wasn't there. He began to think that the girls back at the dairy, knowing how much he yearned to see Jean, were playing a joke on him. He wondered around the area for more than twenty minutes before coming to conclusion that she wasn't there. As he hung his head and began to walk away he heard a voice but didn't see anyone. "Hey" she whispered from the shadows of one of the storage tanks. Jackson looked around acting as if he did not recognize her voice. "Over here" she said, drawing Jackson's attention and gesturing for him to come out of sight where she was standing. With in seconds Jackson found himself standing in front of her. She shyly looked up at him. "Did you miss me?"

"Yes . . . yes I did", he answered. They both stood awkwardly in silence for what seemed to be an eternity.

"Please touch me," she said. Jackson reached out and gently grabbed her hand.

"I'm sorry" she said.

"For what?" he asked.

"For not being able to write you back or see you for such a long time. I tried so hard to get you a message but everything I sent to you they found and punished me by keeping me in confinement. I've been going crazy trying to see you before I leave".

"What do you mean leave, where you go'n?"

"They've found a relative in Washington D.C. that wants to take me in. I'm supposed to leave in another three weeks. I was so afraid that I would never see you again."

"I wanted to see you too . . . I had just about given up. I thought you didn't like me for some reason, but I kept hoping I'd see you and get another chance to say something that might win you. And now here I am trying to think of something that I can do or say to just get you to know that I exist. I just don't know what," he said as he hunched his shoulders in his boyish way.

"Don't say anything, just put your arms around me and hold me again. I've been here since I turned twelve. So many times I thought that I was dreaming and that I would awaken and find myself back home. So many times I've thought that someone would come here and take me away. I've missed my mom and dad so desperately. I just want somebody to love me. I think I've forgotten what it's like." Jackson positioned himself directly in front of her and gently grabbed her shoulders. Though very young, Jackson's shoulders were as broad as or broader than the average adult. He paused for a moment and looked into her eyes as if he were looking for some message or a signal of what he should do next. She waited with her eyes latched onto his. "Please," she said, "please kiss me." Jackson still hesitated.

"Please" she said, this time louder. Jackson leaned forward and placed his lips against her forehead. He lowered his arms down and around her back.

"Please" she said again.

"Please what?" Jackson asked. "What do you want me to do?." She suddenly stood on her toes and rapped her arms around the back of his neck. Without another word she moved her lips against his and just as quickly she settled back down on her heels with her eyes still closed and her lips still poised for another kiss. She eagerly waited for his response. Jackson stood dumbfounded with his own eyes closed and wondering why she stopped. When he finally opened his eyes, there she was beautifully waiting for him to pull her tightly to him and to never let her go again. Finally, he bent down and lifted her up into his arms. Instinctively he placed his lips against hers.

"Please" she said again between his boyish but still ravishing kisses.

"Please, please, please feel me, feel me all over and don't stop until I tell you to." Jackson was quickly learning what God-given passion was all about. As he caressed her he felt her legs weakening and causing her to rely upon him to hold her up. He gently let her fall towards the ground allowing her to pull him down with her. Gently . . . , gently . . . , magically they learned the natural meaning of love and affection. After lying together for awhile Jackson's attention was drawn to her face as she lie against his shoulder with her eyes closed. She laid there beside him clutching him against her as if she would never let go. She was stunningly beautiful. He knew that there was a mutual bond between them that would never be broken. And that he would never allow anything to come between them. When she was about to awaken she stretched her body like a child, smiled and slightly opened her eyes.

"I've got to leave you," she whispered. Jackson quickly sat up and began to speak. She placed her fingers against his lips stopping him from responding.

"One last time," she said, "I'm saying please; please love me for all the days that you exist."

"I will, and I'll find you, this I promise".

They continued to talk until it was nearly dark, knowing that by that time someone or everyone must be looking for the both of them; they didn't care. When they did decide that they had to rejoin the world she forced herself away from him. She was in tears and he wore a pleading look that said, don't leave yet. She knew she had to say goodbye. As she walked away she kept turning towards him and waving again and again until she was completely out of his view. When she was finally out of sight, he whispered . . .

'I love you,' she whispered, 'I always will.'.

Chapter 9

A story: 'Robin Hood's train robbery'

"One day when I was still about ten or eleven, six of us was picking apples in the rear section of the orchard that was located just down the street from our homes. The orchard was sometimes a loafing place during the summer months. We met there often to pick apples to sell for a quarter and some times just to have apple battles. As usual the train came through about 3:00 p.m. There were times we would stop whatever we were doing and just sit on the banks of the rail-way and watch the train go by. It was always exciting to see and feel the ground vibrate from the metal monster roaring through non-stop. At times we could count as many as eighty boxcars clanging and swaying their way through the small Coverdale valley. There were many times that I dreamed that the train would someday accidentally drop something of value so we could take it home and rave to our friends about our luck. This summer day the train stopped on the curve between the local lumber yard and the orchard. As far as we could see in both directions, all of the box cars sat idle as if after all these years they had finally come to their resting place. We watch for nearly and hour. There wasn't any movement or noise coming from the train, nor were there any railroad men in sight.

"Let's open a door," the suggestion was offered by none other than me. "Let's just see what's inside."

"I'm game" was Eddie's reply. A short glance at everyone seemed to confirm a lot of hesitation; but yet a willingness, as long as I went first. I took a pocketknife and snapped the little metal clip holding the door lever. After fumbling awhile with the mechanism I pulled, first upward and then outwards and the door latch let the huge iron door open. My eyes lit up as we gawked at the all the boxes filled with fine furniture; couches, chairs, coffee tables all just sitting and inviting us to take our pick. A few of the boys had began to look around and find pieces of furniture that they thought would be small enough to carry back home. Suddenly! there was a hard jolting yank that pulled the train for about eight feet and came back to a stop. Half-scared, we jumped off the train and ran for cover. After a short time we slowly gained enough courage to walk back closer to the box car with the side door still wide open. I wanted to go back in and get at least a couple of boxes off no matter what might be in side.

"Let's go back in."

"No, they might pull off and take us with them," my friend Gregg said.

"We can jump off if it moves" I said.

"What if the rail man comes while we're inside and closes the door on us?"

"Ah man stop be'n a sissy, there ain't nobody come'n" I said "plus we can see if anyone's come'n before we go in. You and Vance go that way and me and Eddie can go the other way to make sure the rail guys aren't come'n,"

Me and Eddie ran towards the front of the train for a couple hundred feet without seeing anyone. There seemed to be nothing moving up ahead so we went back and resumed our devilment. I had a brainy idea that might give us a little time for our furniture-shopping spree. With a metal bar that was attached to the end of one of the box cars I pried the retaining rings lose and managed to disconnect the coupling and safety pin that held boxcars together. About ten minutes later the train slammed into gear. Away it went, the front end of the train left the rest of the train right where it had been with our furniture still inside. I'm not sure if they were still in Pennsylvania when they discovered that they had left about twenty or so box cars behind. All of us shopped and picked furniture for family and friends. We must have unloaded those boxcars for at least five hours, carrying our bounty up the embankment and into the orchard for hiding. The next morning the train was gone. We gave all of the furniture away over the following few days. Every one in our hood had new furniture. We had gotten away with the biggest train robbery in Pennsylvania. The train heist became a legendary happening in our little town and was talked about for years to come."

"All man you just lie'n" stated one of Jackson's faithful listeners.

"Tell us another story" another listener asked.

A story: 'Hanging on a rope'

"Well . . . a while later after I turned thirteen, there was our Grocery store caper. On this night we decided to bring home the bacon. This particular food store was break-in proof, concrete walls, alarms on all doors, and no rear or side windows. It was a Sunday just before dark. Eddie Brooks and I decided to challenge the new mega store. After plotting about not only how to get in, but how to get food out, we located a hatch door in the center of the roof. The climb to the top was easy. There was an attached metal ladder that led directly to the round shape metal rooftop. Once on top we lifted the hatch, which was held down by only a bolt lock. The problem was the hatch door was in the center of the ceiling and about thirty feet from the floor. After pondering the problem for a few days we returned with enough bull rope to reach and let us down onto the floor. After tying the rope off on a metal ring welded to the roof, we began our decent. The master plan was to stack meat for home and cartons of cigarettes to sell in a couple of grocery carts and wheel them out and into a wooded area until the police left. We knew that as soon as the door was opened from the inside the burglar alarm would sound bringing the local police. I climbed down the rope first, reaching the floor about the same time that a set of headlights from a police car began shining into the storefront window. It was probably just a routine check. The store was slightly lit, even though it was closed for business. With the car lights seemingly shining directly in my face, I thought I was spotted. I fell to the floor immediately knowing I had no way out. Looking up I could see Eddie Brooks half way down the rope about fifteen feet off the floor. As I lay behind a pickle barrel in the center of the isle, I tried to bring Eddie's attention to our dilemma motioning him to hold still. The front glass windows were about ten feet tall and at least two feet off of the ground. Due to the light frost covering the glass I could not clearly see out. I could distinguish the car lights and the fact that it was a police car. The spotlight had popped on and a policeman was calmly walking toward the glass. With Eddie still dangling from the rope and me trying to hold still and not be seen, the officer used his hand in an attempt to wipe off the frost in a small area so he could look in. With the frost on the inside the wiping was to no avail. I could clearly see him now cupping his hands against the glass and trying again to peer inside. He apparently could not see in. I took a deep sigh of relief thinking; maybe he hadn't spotted either of us. By now Eddie was attempting to climb back up the rope and not getting very far. As he climbed a few feet upward he slid downward another five feet, still dangling in full view and getting very tired in his effort. The policeman, having no luck where he was standing, began to walk towards the left front of the store where the glass was unfrosted and clear. The clear glass on both doors and a glass transom up above; put Eddie in full view. Desperate, I stood up and gestured for Eddie to come down the rope, now! He was still climbing up as best he could and getting nowhere. I began to softly yell; "come down now or he'll see you." He was still heading upward where he finally lost his grip and fell to the floor just as the policeman reached the clear glass and was now looking inside. Just as it appeared that he didn't see us and was about to turn and leave, he paused and looked up, spotting the hanging rope. I remember saying, "Shit we're busted!" We stood upright and now, in full view began running as fast as we could toward the rear door. The officer fired two shots through the glass and stood yelling. "Stop right there." Well, we ran faster, hitting the rear double doors in full stride. The doors opened slightly but a heavy metal linked chain had been looped between the two panic bars as an additional locking device. The impact of the doors coming back at us threw us to the floor. After quickly getting up, we slammed against the doors again, only to find that not only the chain was still doing its job, but also that, the officer had come all the way to the back of the store and was waiting outside in a crouched posture ready to shoot again while shaking and yelling, "Hold it right there." The doors slammed shut again in our face with the officer still yelling hold it and come out with your hands up. Speaking through the closed door Eddie began to inform the officer that he was coming out. I was already in full stride again and now heading for the front of the store. Reaching the front door, which had been shot out by the policeman, I exited with Eddie right on my tail and the policeman still at the back door demanding our surrender. With no where to run but into an open parking lot, we foolishly jumped into the idling police car and found ourselves driving off. Red lights flashing, we headed toward home. Looking at each other without saying a word, we realized we had truly just dodged a bullet . . . Good night."

Jackson told story after story, as said, most was based upon exaggerated truth and some were tales that Jackson himself had heard as a kid. Others were just plain old lies that he learned to tell to keep their interest and respect. No one seemed to care, the stories were much better than the bad memories that most of the boys had of their own. Just like his older brother, he learned to start the tales off with, "then there was the time we did this or that." No matter what his stories were they always seem to be worth hearing.

"All my stories aren't bad you know. I can tell you about things that happened back home that was good things. Funny things did happen too."

A story: 'Ruth shot the rooster/ Pudd'n Head's fish

"Let me tell you about the time as a kid no more than six years old. I went fishing with Papa Jones (nick named, Pudd'n Head) and Mr. Eddie Ray (nick named, Lighting). They were both older men that had lived across the street from each other for years. Every once in a while they would take me along mainly to send me to the bait store. Mr. Eddie Ray was a tall thin man with a pointed nose, in fact, though he was dark skinned, all of his facial features were white. Papa Jones was the typical looking older man with a big belly and with a cigar always tucked in his mouth but never lit. It seemed that he just held it in his mouth to chew on it. He looked a lot like Amos of the Amos and Andy show. Anyway, . . . even if the fish weren't biting neither of them wanted to leave there rods unattended just in case the big one decided to bite the moment they walked away. It is said that a real fisherman never wants to take his eye off of his line. These two guys sat for hours sipping their bottles and staring at their rods while lying about any and every thing they talked about. It never made any sense to me. Some times they would fish for hours and not get a nibble, yet if they got up to take a piss they constantly looked over their own shoulder in fear that they would miss a bite. And then they would sit back down for more hours talking with their eyes still glued to their lines, just in case.

On this one night nothing was biting and Papa Jones began to tell me a story about my momma. He said; "boy you see that scar under your left eye?" I responded with a head shake in acknowledgment. "Do you know how you got it?" This time I shook my head no. "Well it was like this, when you were about two years old you wondered out the back door of your daddy's house and through the neighbors fence and into his chicken coupe. Well . . . as everyone knows chickens run when people come around and sho-nuff when you got in the coupe they scattered and went' a run'n. Be'n a little bold, like you were, you went'ta chase'n them chickens like you was try'na catch one for food. Well . . . all the chickens just jumped and clucked in a panic try'n to stay out of your reach. Well . . . don't you know that all of a sudden Mr. Grigg's big old rooster came out of the hen house, I guess to see what all of the commotion was about, and he laid eyes on you and seen how small you were and decided he was gon'na fight you off of his hens. Well . . . you didn't know no better, you just went after that rooster with both hands fling'n and you was just'ta grin'n. Well that old rooster just slowly walk up to you and paused right in front of you wait'n to see what you was gon'na do. You, be'n just a baby, didn't know the rooster was about to pluck at-chew, so you just kept a come'n. Just when you bent forward to pick the rooster up it went'ta peck'n at your head. Now . . . you let the rooster go . . . but it was too late. He just kept on a pluck'n. By now folks began to realize what was happening and went'ta run'n and try'n to get into the coupe and save you but they couldn't get in fast enough. That ole rooster just tried to pluck your eyes out. But you was fight'n him like you knew what you was do'n. When they finally got-chew out you was'a bleed'n like crazy around your eyes. Well . . . bout that time Ruth pulled up in her car and took one look at-chew. I saw her eyes open up in a fury. She handed you to somebody and went up them steps in a hurry and came back down with Chuck's shotgun in hand. Wud'n no body gon'na get in her way that's for sure, not with that shot gun cocked and ready. Well . . . she went out back and up into that hen house and went'ta shoot'n every thing that moved. The chickens, the rooster, the ducks, I mean every thing; she shot ev-ver-ry-thing and loaded up and was shoot'n some more. Finally, she ran out of shells and somebody carefully walked up to her and grabbed the shotgun. "Now", she said, and with a pouted and angry mouth, she went on to say, "no body better not ever touch my baby cause I'll kill them too." They, Poppa Jones and Mr. Eddie Ray, both gave out a hardy laugh and said "Aint nobody messed with Ruth or none of her babies since."

By now, Papa Jones had gotten a little hungry and decided to walk with me up to the bait store while Mr. Eddie Ray watched the lines. They were both pretty drunk as they had been hitting their pints of whisky in their usual ritual of taking a swig after every cast of the line. They always said it was for luck even though neither one of them seemed to have much luck with catching any fish. I think I caught more fish than both of them with just a line and hook that they given me to drag along the shoreline. Anyway . . . while we were gone Mr. Eddie Ray had dozed off to sleep and sure enough a big carp got on his line and pulled his rod into the water. He never heard a thing. When Papa Jones and I returned he stirred a little and realized that one of his rods had been taken into the water. He tried his best to blame it on one of us for taking so long but that was weak and he gave up quickly saying, "dam-it that was one of my favorite rods. Oh well, its gone now and there's nothing I can do about it." "That's right, there's nothing you can do about it but learn how to fish," Papa Jones sarcastically said. Then he gave a hardy laugh that reflected just how stupid he thought it was for someone to go to sleep and lose not only the only fish that took the bait all night, but to lose his rod also, he shook his head with one more devious grin just as his own bobber slapped hard against his rod letting him know that he had a big fish on the line. Papa Jones's whole expression changed immediately as he grabbed his rod and yank good and hard to set the hook. Much to his surprise he knew he had hooked a big one. The rod bent over. The drag wined like a baby as the big fish pulled hard for its freedom. Papa Jones slipped to the ground spitting out his unlit cigar but held the rod firmly. He was not about to let this one get away. The big carp swam from side to side. It ran deep and tried to pull away but Papa Jones just tightened up his line and wined the fish closer and closer. "Get the net," he yelled with a boyish grin on his face. "This is the biggest fish in the world and I got it". Mr. Eddie Ray had the net ready he was just as excited as Papa Jones to see what size fish that could pull and fight so hard and for so long. After another ten minutes of fighting, the big fish finally began to yield and give Papa Jones the upper hand.

"Net'm, got-dam-it get the net on'm before he breaks the line!" he shouted to Mr. Eddie Ray. By now Papa Jones had fallen a couple times and had gotten back up, he fell once more, it looked for a moment as if the fish was pulling him into the water but he still held his ground. Finally, Mr. Eddie Ray swooped the net down and brought in the thirty inch carp. A small crowd had gathered around just to see the size of the now landed fish. Papa Jones snatch the net away from Mr. Eddie Ray and pulled his trophy out and held it as high into the air as his strength would allow him, so everyone could see. It was his moment of glory. He had waited a long time to show up Mr. Eddie Ray and wasn't about to let this moment pass quickly. When he sat the fish down to remove the hook he noticed that there were two hooks in the fish's mouth. He removed his hook and pulled on the other line finding that it led back into the water. He continued to pull the line until the line revealed that it was still attached to another fishing rod.

"That's my fish'n rod!" Mr. Eddie Ray shouted as he grabbed it up out the water. He reeled in his line and there he stood with the hook of his line embedded into the fish that Papa Jones had just reeled in.

"This is my fish," Mr. Eddie Ray calmly said.

"Like hell it is, that's my fish, I caught it and brought it in, everybody here seen me do it. And, I think that's now my rod, since I'm the one that pulled it out of the lake."

"So what,' Mr. Eddie Ray said. "I caught it first and my hook is still in it's mouth everybody can see that. Even as stupid as you are, you can see that; and that makes it mine."

"Nigga, no it aint! Not only is it my fish but it's my rod since I pulled it out of the water where you had lost it.

"What?" Mr. Eddie Ray yelled back as he put his nose right against Papa Jones's. "Nigga I'll kill you if you don't get out'ta my face, this is my fish and you know it."

They swung at each other for a while and then pulled out their pocket knives and circled each other for another twenty minutes. I got tired of watching them staggering and swinging without ever hitting one another. While they were busy almost fighting, I felt sorry for the fish. I took out the hook and push it back into the water. At that point they finally stopped fighting. They both flopped to the ground and swore that they would never take me fish'n again." . . .

"That was funny, I'm like'n your stories more and more", Said a listening voice.

A story: 'Boulevard dog'

"One early Sunday morning just before Christmas, Eddie and I went shopping. All of Coverdale was headed to the local church for Sunday school. Eddie Brooks and I headed out for a days work on the newly built industrial boulevard. Industrial Boulevard was a commercial strip of property near Coverdale. It was developed on a piece of land previously used as a red dog dump for the coal mine that runs underneath our little town. The first stage of development began in the late fifties. At this time there were approximately twenty newly constructed commercial businesses just behind the dump. The dump was used as a barrier between the up and coming businesses and our old coal mining community. It was the invisible fence between the poor and the not so poor. In some folks minds it was the invisible fence between the blacks and the whites. Though a lot of folks were employed there, not one person from Coverdale was ever fortunate enough to get a job on the boulevard. Most of us were too dark-skinned to qualify for employment. Trying not to be obvious, we started our adventure under by taking my dog for a walk. It was about 9:a.m. as the two us and my dog, named Nevada, headed out waving at our friends and Sunday School go'ers with a flashlight and screwdriver in our pockets. Our challenge for this day was to nose around as many buildings as we could in just one day. Our adventure was planned under the disguise of taking my dog for a walk and using Nevada as our watchdog. We managed to crawl under locked gates and fences and to pry doors open to see what we could find inside. We tried sending Nevada in first to make sure there was no guard dog inside. That didn't work at all, because Nevada was not a fellow burglar, he was the big chicken. He only turned right around to get back out. None-the-less, we proceeded into each property one after another looking for junk and any valuables that may be worth taking so we could give them to our friends and family as Christmas gifts. I don't remember what our take was by the end of the day. I do know that we did successfully reach our goal of entering every fenced property on the boulevard in one day. The following day just after school, we found our old familiar friend and captain of the Bethel Park police, Jack Dabney, at my house talking to my mother. The sight of the police car in my yard was alarming. Mr. Dabney often came by my house to talk with my mother about her 'numbers business', and to have some of my Mom's homemade beer. But this time I had a gut feeling that his visit was about me and Eddie and the Boulevard caper. As I entered the house it was confirmed that this visit was different. There were two other officers with him and they were asking for the whereabouts of my Uncle Watson. My Uncle Watson was an x-Korean war hero that was always in trouble with the law and he occasionally visited us from the city. I heard Mr. Dabney tell my mother "Ruth," he said, "there is no other dog with paws this big in all of Pa. and we found dog prints in the buildings all over the boulevard. We know it had to be Watson." He must have been right, I was only twelve at the time; I couldn't have done it. My Dad was at work and everyone knows he's super honest, he couldn't have done it. My Mom couldn't have done it. My brother Larry was out of town, he couldn't have done it. The dog couldn't have done it alone; so it must have been Uncle Watson. When they finally picked up my Uncle Watson, he said, "I didn't do it . . . I'm afraid of that dog!" and sure enough, when Jack Dabney escorted him up near Nevada, he tried to bite their legs off. Jack Dabney told my Dad, "You need to do something about that dog Chuck, no one can get near him, not even you. What good is he?" My dad replied, "He likes Jackson" . . . That was the last I heard anything of the 'boulevard caper' and to this day they haven't found the dog burglar.

A story: 'Can't stop lying

"Once in 1955 when I was nine, my dad took the whole family to Versharens. Versharens was a huge nursery and variety store located across from South Park entrance. Although they sold mostly plants, shrubs and pottery, they had a section of toys and sports equipment. The main part of the store was a brick structure that was once one of the Isley's ice cream stores that was located at the corner of South Park road and route 88. The rear or side section of the building was made up of rows of metal and wood props covered with tarp. On this day I spent my whole time playing in the toy section as my dad shopped for pots and plants for his garden. My younger brother and sister, Chuckie and Nancy and I had found a happy world of playing with the plastic military soldiers until it was time to leave. That night, in the wee hours of the night or at least after 10:00 p.m., I convinced Chuckie that we should sneak and walk to Versharen's and play with the plastic toys . . . no one would know, in fact, no one would care. Chuckie was only about six years old. I wasn't really sure he could walk that far without getting tired; but, what we both knew for sure was that we didn't have these toys at home and we wouldn't be getting them or any toys until at least Christmas, which was a lifetime away, it was only

July. The walk to Versharen's in the middle of the night was uneventful. No one seemed to pay attention to a nine and six year old sneaking into the open end of the store. We played with any and every toy we chose. As the night drew on, we finally headed home with our pockets stuffed with toys. Apparently we were missed. We weren't far from home when we spotted our father's car headed towards us; "he seen us!" We dashed between two buildings on South Park road, behind Ann's bar. We ducked into the knee-high grass as his car pulled onto the gravel driveway. Chuckie and I were about ten feet apart lying on the ground hiding in the high grass and hoping he didn't see us. At first he drove his car right by us and we thought we had gotten away. Then, he slammed on his brakes and made the loud noise that tires make when they're kicking gravel against the bottom of the car. Our father got out and loudly said, "All right, I see you, come out those weeds right now!" At first I didn't move and neither did Chuckie; then again, this time even louder, "Damn it boy, come out of there right now, I see you!" I knew he couldn't possibly see us and stayed put, but Chuckie stood up and began walking to the car saying, "Jackson made me do it, I didn't want to". Immediately I stayed low and began crawling towards home. Once out of view, I stood straight up and ran like blazes for Cherry Street. Looking back and down over the hill, I could see the headlights of the car and my dad walking back and forth looking for me in the weeds and still yelling "I see you". Once home, I sneaked back through my window and climbed into bed as fast as I could. I could hear my mother pacing downstairs saying, "I'm gon'na tear his little ass up, where could they be at this time of night?" I could hear the anger in her voice and yet some concern that Chuckie was with me and something may have happened to him. About this time, my dad walked in with Chuckie tucked under his right arm; "Jackson made me!" he kept saying again and again. "Put him down, where's Jackson?"

"I don't know ma; he made me go".

I was peeking through my cracked bedroom door and trying to hear what was going on.

"Where were you boy?" she asked Chuckie.

"Jackson took me somewhere momma, are you going to whoop me?"

"No, just sit down, where's Jackson?" she repeated.

"O-o-l, you gon'na git it", I looked down to see the origin of this sassy girlie voice, "Momma, Jackson's' up here look'n through his door, you gon'na-git-it now boy", my sister Nancy said again. I jumped back into bed as if I had been home all the time.

"Why you wake'n me up girl, with that noise?" I said. Nancy pushed my bedroom door open.

"Momma wants you right now!"

"Get down here you little bastard, don't make me come up those steps!" Acting as though I had been asleep, I came out of my room and onto the steps yawning and stretching my arms.

"What ma, what I do now?"

"You know what'chu did". She had my dad's mining belt in her hand. She grabbed Chuckie by the back of his shirt with one hand and whacked him five or six times. Chuckie yelled as if he was going to die. I knew I was in trouble, he never gets whooped.

"Get down here!" My sleepy acting wasn't working, but I wasn't giving up.

"Nancy just woke me up ma, I was asleep".

"Don't lie to me boy, get down here!" She was getting madder and I was still sticking to my story.

"I didn't go with Chuckie ma, did I Chuckie? Tell momma the truth."

"Yes you did, you made me go too!" Momma gave him one more whack and told him to get upstairs. Screaming and rubbing his butt, he ran pass me and up the steps. I could see the joy in his eyes as he passed me with a grin on his face. He survived, now it was my turn. "Get down here right now!" I had been slowly descending one step at a time, and with each step I was still making my plea.

"Ma, I swear, I was sleep, ask anybody, they'll tell you, Nancy wasn't I sleep, didn't you just wake me up?"

"No!" she said, in a signifying way. "You didn't take me, I told momma, now!"

"Right now boy, you're making it worst." My mother was now standing beside a chair with the belt in one hand; she pointed with the other.

"Lay down on the chair," she said. I made one more plea.

"I swear to you momma, I was asleep." It wasn't working. "I love you, I love you momma!" That wasn't working either.

"Get your little ass over the chair, right now," she screamed. I immediately laid down on the chair, back-wards with my butt down, my stomach up, I lay arching my back and holding on to the back of the chair to keep from falling. My mother nearly cracked a smile at me now facing the ceiling and still sticking to my lie. "Turn over boy, you know what I meant!" I turned half way over on one side; she touched my leg with her hand to assist my turn. I screamed out in pain even though she had yet to strike the first whack.

"Ma, don't whoop me, I'll tell everything . . . It was Larry and Chuckie, I was sleep." With that last lie she began lashing me unmercifully with my daddy's mining belt. She paused after what seemed like hundreds of hits and said, "don't you move, um not done wit-chu yet". Her asthma was causing her to pant and breath real hard, and then she said,

"Don't you lie to me ever again, now where were you?"

"Okay momma", I said, with a fake hick-cupping sound coming with each word. "I-I-I'll tell you the truth momma, if I do are you still gon'na whip me some more?"

"Tell the truth boy!" my daddy said, I guess he wanted to get this all over with. "Okay . . . I-I-I told Larry and Chuckie not to go down to Versharen's but they went anyway". I don't know how much longer the beating lasted, but I do remember she stopped and rested for a while . . . at least three times . . . and commenced again until her arm was too tired to continue. I never admitted leaving my room that night. Every time she asked, I lied. She gave me whippings at least once a week trying to get me to tell the truth. I couldn't, I couldn't tell the truth because I thought that if I told the truth it would mean that I had lied to her in the beginning, and I just refused to be caught in a lie especially since I really didn't actually get caught . . . Good night guys."

"No, no, wait, Pittsburgh, you tell us a lot of stories but what actually happen that got you sent here? I want to know because it seems that the things you done were child like and innocent and that can't be right. Just tell us the one story that took you down."

"Okay," Jackson said, "this is the way that one nasty day started and went on to put us away.

A story: 'Jackson goes to jail'

It was on my birthday, December 14, 1959 Bethel Park's chief of police, nicked named Fats, had made a deal with Bobby Perry on a felony charge. He, being Bobby Perry, could stay out of prison if he could deliver a certain packet of information located in a safe at a state liquor store warehouse in Bridgeville. He was told any money or liquor was his to keep. All he needed to do was bring a packet marked state liquor control board from the safe to Fat's home located just across the street from Pitt grove in South Park. Bobby was made aware that the building was well alarmed, both doors and windows. The chief was aware of my mode of operandi of cutting through block walls without setting off an alarm system and had convinced Bobby that his charge would be dropped if he could pull this off. Bobby met with Eddie Brooks, Billy Muldon and myself. He gave us three hundred dollars each for spending money and asked us to accompany him for a ride to scope out a warehouse where we could make a lot more money and bring home some sellable goods. He drove us to Bridgeville in his 1954 Cadillac; I felt like a mobster, of sort, that I had seen so many times on television. In broad daylight we parked across the street from the warehouse. There stood a very inconspicuous building built of concrete block with no windows and well off the main road. It was the only building on a lot just across a set of railroad tracks. It had two docks, no parking lot or outside lights were apparent. Bobby's deal to us: using his truck, we were to bring him the safe out of the warehouse, in exchange for another three hundred dollars each up front and the use of his truck to haul all the liquor we wanted to keep. It sounded too good to be true, I thought to myself, we're finally going to be big time gangsters. This was my fourteenth birthday. We arrived at the warehouse just after dark, about 5:45 p.m. Snow was lying on the warehouse grounds, undisturbed, indicating that there had been no vehicle activity since the last snow fall several days before. We found it very odd that there hadn't been any traffic in or out of this driveway or dock. The warehouse appeared to have been vacant for quite some time. The overhead dock doors looked as if they hadn't been open for years. The front door was dirty. Road dust had collected at the bottom of the door, all the cracks and ledges were caked with dirt. There were no lights on inside or out. No phone lines or outside alarm bell was anywhere to be found. The front door was made of wood with an old skeleton key type lock and obviously no alarm. I remember wondering if we could have somehow plotted the wrong building, but there was no other building in sight. We talked for a moment. "Something was wrong, this is much too easy." Wiping a clear spot in a glass panel beside the door, we used a flashlight to look inside. Again, it appeared that no one had been inside for years, dust laid on everything, and it truly appeared abandoned. Eddie backed off the door and gave one hard kick, the door flew open and we were in. The dusty boxes in the front area were empty. There were stacks of papers and books on the shelves from floor to ceiling. We approached a second interior door with caution; still looking for the burglar alarm that we were told would be there . . . The door was locked and seemed to be braced from the other side and it appeared to be armed. We decided we should kick a hole in the plaster wall right next to the door to avoid any type of booby-trap. We were now feeling puzzled. What is this place and why is it so conveniently easy? Entering the next room through our newly made doorway, we could see that the door was braced with crossing boards nailed to the frame. The only other way in or out was the docks overhead doors that appeared to be locked from the inside and jammed with a piece of board so it could not be opened from the outside. It was apparent that no one had been here for quite some time and whoever wanted in, would have to break in just as we did. This was very mysterious. Shining our flashlight, we could see stacks upon stacks of cases of liquor, all kinds, neatly arranged by their name brands and again appearing dusty and undisturbed. We slapped each others hands with excitement and thinking big time. Eddie and Billy began stacking boxes of liquor at the dock door, while I explored looking for the safe. There was no other office or partitioned area to be found. I walked from front to rear through the box lined aisles, looking for a room that may house the sought after safe. I remember again thinking, something is wrong with this; it's much too easy. Later this would be the demise of a lifetime. Not finding a safe; I proceeded to help with the loading of the truck. We covered about thirty cases of liquor of random brands, pulled down the doors and headed for Bethel. We drove to a rear alley way behind my house and unloaded the cases into our unused out-house, where they wouldn't be found and headed for Bobby's house where we found him and his girl friend laid back listening to jazz. "Where's the safe?" he asked.

I explained that there was no safe in the building and that the building seemed to be vacant but loaded with liquor. We drove back here to see what you wanted us to do". He seemed to be excited about the liquor, but more concerned about the safe. He wanted us to wait while he made a call. On the phone, he informed someone, I assumed the police chief, that there was no safe. He hung up quickly and said. Let's go, I'll follow you guys there in the caddie". He paused and made one more call to someone named Sam. I heard him tell Sam about the liquor.

After writing a couple brand names on a scratchpad, he hung up and said to us," Sam wants to buy as many cases as you guys can bring to him, preferably Canadian whiskey, he is willing to pay $3.00 a bottle, you guys keep $2.00 a bottle and give me a buck, it's a deal?" We didn't answer we just slapped hands sealing the deal and led the way back to the warehouse. It was still early evening; I would guess about 7:30 or 8:00 p.m. when we arrived. When we got inside, Eddie and Billy began loading the Canadian whiskey at the dock door. I followed Bobby to what appeared to be closet door up front where we had first entered. There was a thin narrow winding set of steps leading up to a loft on top of the front office. Unlike the rest of the building, this room seemed to have been recently in use; it had a phone and lights, which Bobby turned on. There were stacks of active and recently dated papers with stock numbers and dollar signs and just as it was described, a small safe sitting in the corner, clean and inviting.

On one side of the room there was a door marked danger! While Bobby was looking at and tinkering with the safe, I carefully opened the door, still expecting a burglar alarm. The door led to the back of the warehouse but without steps, just a ten foot drop to the concrete floor below and perhaps used to bring in the safe and definitely the only way to get it out.

The two of us pushed the safe over to the door, "Look out below!" we shouted. The safe crashed hard against the concrete floor and just as everything else seemed too easy to be true. The safe door opened on impact, spilling envelopes and papers onto the floor including, very familiar to me, numbers slips. There was no cash to be found. Bobby gathered all the papers put them in a bag and gave us a phone number and address of this man name Sam. He left the building, leaving us alone with our bounty.

The truck was loaded, three boxed high and four boxes wide from the cab to the tailgate, in total about 75 boxes of nothing but Canadian whiskey. The three of us jumped into the truck and headed for the North side to meet Sam for our money. Kind of smiling ear to ear, we crossed the West end Bridge, just off of Route 51 and made two right turns past the old dairy and into an alley behind a row of attached brick homes. The man named Sam was waiting on the rear porch. He directed us into a small garage, where we unloaded and stacked the boxes. We settled on a new bargain price of $75.00 per case, which should have given us just over $5,000. Sam only had $3,000, explaining that he didn't know we were bringing so much liquor. We didn't care; we were finally in the big time. Sam asked if we had anymore. Eddie responded with, "Do you have anymore money?" Sam then plotted our demise. He said, "Bring me another load; I'll have the $5,000 here, plus the other $2,000 when you get back".

We were headed back to our liquor warehouse. We stopped at home along the way and stashed well over $3,000. And some whiskey for ourselves and continued on our way. We drove the back way to Bridgeville, which was about a fifteen-minute drive. Entering Bridgeville, we crossed a single land bridge less than a mile from the warehouse, that's when all hell broke lose. Apparently, after we left Sam, he decided to move the liquor he had purchased, into a bar he owned at another location on the North Side; while doing so, he was pulled over by a city policeman on a routine traffic stop. The officers had discovered the whiskey and arrested Sam and two other adults, who of course, ratted out, not only our description and type of truck but also that we were headed back somewhere in Bridgeville for another load. They didn't want to go down for burglary, so they took the fall for receiving stolen goods, which is the lesser crime.

Meanwhile, we were unaware of the arrest and driving along as happy as a lark thinking of our $7,000 to come.

As we reached the center of the bridge, a police car pulled across blocking the end of the bridge in front of us. Slamming into reverse in an attempt to back off, the rear view mirror showed two more police cars blocking the other end. We were trapped in the center. Guns were drawn and pointed at the three of us. There was no where to run, we were busted . . . That's what got me here."

The next morning . . . "Rise and shine," called out the Morganza guard, "Jackson Thomas Reynolds, report to the main office today at 10:00, here's your pass." He had been there for ten months and this is the first time he had ever been called to the main office.

He hadn't the slightest idea why he was being summoned.

'Maybe I'm going home . . . ' at 9:30 a.m. he headed unescorted for the administration building. He hadn't been there since the night El-Tez was killed during the attempted escape.

To this date, he wasn't sure if they ever found his body. He had asked his mother several times, 'had she heard anything from his family,' she never answered. She really didn't know his (El-Tez's) family that well and Jackson guessed that she really didn't want to talk about it. Jackson missed him a lot, but he had no idea what, if anything, he could do. There was never any information about him or the break-out attempt mentioned at Morganza and he guessed that there shouldn't be.

When he reached the main office he was told to have a seat. Nuns were scurrying back and forth, just busy doing whatever nuns do. "Please come in uh . . . Jackson Thomas, right?" He must have been the head priest or the main man in charge.He sat in a big leather chair loaded with little metal studs. Every wall and shelf was filled with books and the window had a full view of the creek that he once attempted to cross.

"Sit down Jack," he said, as if he knew him. "We've been watching you since you first arrived here," he said, while flipping through an open file. "You've been good for the other boys here. Everyone seems to like you including the guards.

We really hate to see you leave. If you can stay out of trouble for another sixty days, you're going home. I would like to give you a word of advice. We don't feel that you are a bad boy, you're just opportunistic. You need to focus your energy on your family, go back to school and be someone." Jackson didn't hear much of this short sermon but the word opportunistic stuck in his mind. He wasn't sure he knew what the word meant but he felt it was for him none the less. He was and probably always will be alert to everything passing his way. He made choices instantly; often afraid that he might miss something or someone that will make the difference for him and his family. He knew the difference between hardship and happiness. He knew at this early age that he needed to be the difference. He was determine to never miss an opportunity and to pay attention and not let things pass him by. He thought that with any success he would win the love of his mother, his father and his family, by answering their problems and always having what they needed even before they needed it; whatever it might be. He wanted to protect them from the Mohigans' of the world and at the same time assure them that they would never go hungry. He wanted to be an angel of God, sent here to make life easy. He even thought that, someday, God Himself would need him to fight the evils of the world.

"We're going to let you go home for the weekend to help you and your family reacquaint with each other."

He was confused, he wanted to go home, he had prayed for it, but he had found a new home, a new family and friends who looked up to him; smaller, younger boys who needed his protection. He didn't want to leave and he certainly didn't want to stay. He wanted to be both places. He cried coming, it will be hard not to cry even harder leaving.

His mother picked him up at 3:00 p.m. the first Friday in May, 1961; he was going home. He had been gone for what he thought was a lifetime; in fact, in this short period of time he experienced more excitement than most people experience in their entire life.

His mother said to him, "son your friends and everyone in Coverdale is waiting to see you;. Nancy and Chuckie had planned a welcome home party, I've never seen so much excitement." Jackson was very choked up inside but he wanted to go back, he already began to miss his friends. He could feel those familiar tears slowly sneaking down his cheeks. He quietly asked his mother if he could get out and walk the rest of the way. It was only two more blocks and he was much too shy to be greeted by so many people. He got out and closed the car door as Ruth pulled off and headed down onto Cherry Street. He walked to the top of the street that he had lived on all of his life; he watched as his mother's car pull into the driveway and his little brothers and sisters ran to the car. She must have pointed up the street where Jackson had now come into view. It was like entering the theater back at Morganza. He put on his proud, and what he considered his most handsome face, and strolled hard, swinging one arm and trying to look dangerous. "Who were these people,' he questioned himself. 'Why are they so much smaller now? Why are they all wearing such silly grins? I wish my boys were here with me; Spider and Squirt, we could really make the right entry; demanding respect instead of such silly glee.'

"Jackie" 'no my name is Pittsburgh now,' he thought to himself.

"Jackie!" she repeated, it was Marva Lee Richardson, she lived at the top of the hill where he had made his gangster like entrance. She came up to him, hugged him and kissed him on the cheek. She seemed so glad to see him. By now others were walking to meet him. They were all girls and children, no boys, no men. He didn't know how to wear his look of danger here in this type of crowd. One after another, warm greetings and hugs wore down his gang like appearance. In this whole year he hadn't been touch by anyone or anything other than fist. This was different. Carrie, his hometown sweetheart walked up to him just before he reached home. She kissed him right on the lips. Memories of Morganza began to instantly fade. He was home. He had prayed for it. He had wished for it. "Please don't awaken me like so many times before." After being at Morganza for more than a year, re-adjusting to the normal non-violent lifestyle of Coverdale was like coming to the end of a roller coaster ride.

Chapter 10

The summer of 1961 went by at a snails pace once Jackson was back home. In late August, came high school football season at Bethel Park. The use of all of his stored energy was refocused on the organized violence found in the playing of the game. Our team zipped through the year with a record of 9-0. We had bragging rights to having allowed only one touchdown scored against them during the entire season. This was a new found arena for commitment to unity and camaraderie and a recall of feelings linked to recognition and being special among ones peers.

In May of 1962, Jackson managed to get himself into the thick of things again. School was about to end and he had been advanced to the higher grade of tenth, all seemed well. He had begun to believe that maybe he was normal; maybe he was not black, poor or a juvenile delinquent headed nowhere. He had just exited the junior high location on Park Avenue when he noticed a commotion involving a white boy from Coverdale and three young adults, later confirmed to be from a neighboring Borough. As he approached the four of them, he recognized the one from Coverdale had been pushed to the ground and was being dragged and kicked as he continuously attempted to get upright to flee.

Reacting by instinct, Jackson dropped what he was carrying and found himself pulling one of the assailants to the ground by the back of his shirt, while back handing the biggest of the three. Catching them off guard, he proceeded without a word to assist his fallen homeboy who was now afoot running and heading for home. The two young men were no match for someone fighting back and they were yielding to Jackson who was now taunting, "Come on fight me. Pick on someone your own size." This had now turned to a shoving match with Jackson shoving and the two of them backing down the street saying, "this isn't your fight!" Contrary to the news article of the following day, he was unaware that the boy he had intervened for was affected with hemophilia (a bleeder). He had come to his aide as others had come to his, just to even the odds. The school buses that were filled and lined up bumper to bumper on the other side of the street became his cheering section as the young men continued to yield to his taunting. With the loud cheering, he could not hear the warnings that were now being shouted. Suddenly, he felt a blow from a long metal object striking him on the back just below the ribs.

"Come on nigger, let me show you who the master is." The third attacker said while continuously swinging. The two other opponents had retreated out of reach, as he turned to find the second incoming blow of which he could now see was a stand used for a bumper jack with the jacking mechanism still attached, in the hands of this third attacker. He easily ducked and regained his composure. The boy he was helping was long gone. Now, Jackson was in trouble with two of them behind him and one in front. The third man was again preparing to swing again. Jackson chose to stay focused on the bumper-jack. The metal jack was more than three feet long and very easy to elude. The cheers began to sound like that of a bull fight, each time he swung and missed the sound peeked and fell. Ducking his high swings and jumping backward to the low swings, Jackson avoided contact until a blow came directly at him at about the height of his arm-pit.

Instead of dodging back, He attempted to duct the jack. As he ducked, the jack mechanism at the end of the jack caught him just behind his left ear, knocking him down onto one knee. The two that were unarmed began to kick Jackson as he struggled to keep focusing on the bumper-jack. The racial slurs were pouring out as the three of them beat and kick him nearly into unconsciousness. Jackson didn't know how to give up. He managed to grab the jack preventing anymore blows, while rising to his feet and striking a blow of his own. With jack now in Jackson's hands all three attackers were now retreating due to the oncoming of two of Jackson's friends from Coverdale. According to the cheers from the buses and standing observers, Jackson had indeed won another battle. In the eyes of a friend, Jackson could tell that something was very wrong. He felt the blood gathering around the inside of his belt and seeping down to his hip. His clothes were soaked with his own blood as he now hurriedly walked towards home.

Within the next block the Bethel Park police arrived and arrested Jackson for what was said to be disturbing the peace. At the police station he sat waiting for Captain Jack Dabney. He found himself loosing and regaining consciousness every few seconds. Everyone's voices seemed to be coming through a tunnel and became softer as he sat waiting.

Seemingly, in an instant his mother was now on the scene and standing over him with a frightened look upon her face.

"Got damn-it, I can't believe you have my boy sitting here bleeding like this, I'm taking him right now to a doctor" she said, while lifting Jackson up into her arms. It was the first time Jackson could remember being hugged by his mother and her telling him to just 'hold on son your gon'na be all right".

"Ruth you can't take him, he is under arrest." The policeman's voice fell on the deaf ears as his mother, at four feet eleven inches, dragged Jackson's now limp body to her car.

At the doctor's office, which was less than one mile away, he was very faint but still aware of what was going on around him. "Ruth" the doctor said "we've got to get him to Mercy Hospital right away. The ambulance will be here in a moment."

Jackson could hear the ambulance driver talking, "Please clear the Liberty Tunnels, we're less than two minutes away with a life or death emergency," with that Jackson nodded into unconsciousness. Other than a slight recall of a scratching sound against his skull, he did not awaken until three days later.

Drowsy and unaware of his location, he slowly awakened. He slightly opened his eyes and found himself in one of the many beds at Mercy Hospital and surrounded with flowers and cards. In the background he could hear a radio softly playing a Ray Charles's hit, "I can't stop loving you." Though the music had a sort of country western beat, he found himself enjoying the love lyrics. After the song ended he mysteriously felt that he wasn't alone. He opened and quickly closed his eyes after realizing there was a white girl sitting beside his bed reading a book.

Not remembering why he was there or who she was, he decided to keep his eyes closed and just listen. The next song playing on WAMO, was 'Any day now' by Chuck Jackson, a strong voiced vocalist that was hot at the time. Now this was more like his style of music. As he lies there listening, he began to slightly remember tidbits of what had happened a few days before. He felt the young girl sneakingly grab and gently squeeze his hand, "I love you," she whispered. Jackson was thinking, "she must be overwhelmed by the music. I don't even know who she is." She gently brushed both of his eyebrows with her finger tips as if to lay them back in place. He could feel her breath hitting against his cheek as she apparently moved closer as if to place a kiss. He held still anticipating a kiss upon his cheek knowing that it couldn't hurt even though it would be coming from a stranger. She tenderly brushed her lips across his waiting cheek and much to his surprise, onto his lips. At that moment he opened his eyes and found her blue eyes gazing into his in with a dreamy look upon her face. Her eyes suddenly popped wide open as she realized he was awake. She snapped her head back, "Oh, my God," she said, "your awake, he's awoke!" She let go of his hand and stood up screaming. "You . . . are . . . awake!" she repeated while quickly walking away. In a few moments she returned with Ruth and a nurse at her side. Jackson's mother stood there smiling but resisted giving the hug or the kiss one might expect after such an ordeal. Nonetheless, Jackson knew she was relieved and glad to know he was going to be all right. A nurse suggested that he continue to rest, and that his mother, could now go home and do the same. As he dozed off into a deep sleep, he felt the young girl's hand again caressing his. He heard her tell the nurse, "I'm not leaving until he's alright and I can look into his eyes again" . . . Though Jackson was pleased with the white girl's display of affection, he was still a little uneasy. Jackson never liked being kissed by anyone. He regarded unwelcome kisses as nasty infringements on his privacy. As a six year old he was often taken to a local bar by his fraternal father. His mother made him go along to assure that his father might leave the bar at a reasonable time, maybe sober and maybe with a little money left for food. During the bar binges old drunken women, at least they were old to him, would be sent out to check on Jackson and remark how much he looked like his daddy. Jackson had no idea of what they were talking about. He felt and assumed that Charlie Reynolds was his father and there could be no other. None the less, those women came out to check on Jackson much to often and each time one or another came out, and no one was looking, they took it upon themselves to give Jackson sloppy kisses on his lips causing him to gag and want to throw-up.

In August of 1963, he was himself again and ready to go out into the world of sports like an upstanding young black boy that needed a break. He attempted to rejoin the football team, but was arrogantly denied by the high school coach, due to his injury. Even though Jackson felt ready and able to get back to playing football, the coach didn't feel that he would be good for the team. His opinion was based upon the racial controversy that had begun to thicken not only in Bethel, but all over the country.

The young mystery girl had become like a family member against the wishes of her well to-do parents. Soon after, they moved to Florida, where Jackson later heard that she sadly took her own life. It was said, that she had fallen in love with Jackson and did not want to live without him. Jackson did not recognize a feeling of love for her but after hearing of her death, decided to place her in a place in his heart that he kept sacred and just for her.

He was later proclaimed a hero by the Pittsburgh Courier newspaper for potentially saving the life of the hemophiliac. After a short trial the three white male assailants were found innocent of any wrong doing even though they nearly took Jackson's life. And though the assailants were adults and obviously guilty of something, all charges were dropped. The young man swinging the bumper jack bragged before going out the court room, that, "his family had enough money to buy all the niggers in Bethel Park." Jackson was strangely portrayed as being responsible for the first bit of racial tension in this small coal mining melting pot. This was the first time the true taste of racism was introduced to him. This incident gave Jackson the awareness that racism is a desease that would always be an evil contender of everything good, and that it could cripple the harmony of his hometown and any town across the nation.

To add to the tension, several Coverdale youths, Jackson included, began to become targets for the local police. One night, in early October, armed with a search warrant, the police entered his mother's home. After a thorough search they found twenty cases of liquor between the ceiling rafters. The liquor had been hidden and forgotten years before. His mother and father were threatened with charges that were dismissed when Jackson and Eddie admitted to the crime that they had actually, as said, occurred nearly three years earlier. They charged Jackson and Eddie Brooks with the burglary of the same state liquor store warehouse for the second time.

Without a fair trial, Eddie was sentenced two to four years at the Western Penitentiary for burglary and probation violation. This time Jackson, at age sixteen, was the one sentenced to the state correctional institution at Camp Hill, better known as White-hill. He was sentenced for an indefinite period of time or until he turned eighteen years of age.

PART TWO

Chapter 11

The threat of racial problems in such a small town as Bethel, wasn't going to happen, and with the likes of Jackson and Eddie out of the picture it was a lot less likely. Jackson was again taken from his family and home.

After the sentencing Jackson found himself shackled with a leather belt around the waist and chained from his hands to his feet and locked to the floor of a state vehicle headed for a two and a half-hour drive to Camp Hill PA. The same tears, the same prayers and the same questions of how he got here were his only thoughts as the car pulled into the outer gates of the prison. Here there were armed guard towers and a fifteen-foot barbed wire fence around this huge adult prison. This place was nothing like what he had seen at Morganza. This was a real prison where guards are trained to break a man's spirit. This is a place where you are taught to submit to confinement within iron gated cells that have their own sinks and attached toilets. This is where they put real criminals; a place where they can no longer harm the upstanding businessmen who make an honest living over-charging poor folks for their goods.

"Take off all of your clothes and get into the shower". The shower was in full view of several guards and two inmates that were in charge of fitting prisoners for prison clothing. "Open your mouth", he said, while looking in with a flashlight. "Bend over and put your hands against the rail". Jackson reluctantly did as the guard instructed. He felt cold hands open his ass cheeks as the guard inspected for God knows what with the same handy flashlight. One of the guards asked in a joking way, "ain't we supposed to let the inmates spread their own asses?" "Yea" was the answer, "but this one has such a cute little ass that I couldn't resist". And then the guard said, after a hard smack on Jackson's rear-end, "no luggage in there". He got a burst of laughter from the guards and the inmates that were enjoying the view. "The young boy will be getting luggage soon enough", joked one of the inmates that was standing nearby. Some things just don't change, Jackson thought. This so-called White-hill is bent on making a boy or man's life miserable. He felt the need to immediately re-adjust to a survival mode. I've got to dig deep for the courage that it takes to draw my battle lines with whoever wishes to be against me.

"F—you red neck, you and these nigger bus boys", he said to the guard while pointing at the two inmates that had been staring at his nude body.

"I don't need your shit", said one of the guards while grabbing the front of Jackson's neck and slamming him hard against the wall.

"Look nigger boy, you will do what I say when I say it, you hear me" he said while letting go of his grip. Jackson couldn't afford to let up.

"F—all of you, I ain't scared of your bullshit, this is "Pittsburgh", he shouted, while pounding on his chest in the fashion of a gorilla. A couple of the guards grabbed him and slammed him against the wall again and again. They cuffed his hands behind his back as he began to push back without fear.

"You're going to the hole punk, see how you like that Mr. tough guy."

"So what I can handle anything you got, but when I get out I'm gon'na get both of your faggot asses" he said to the inmates that had found his nakedness so laughable. Jackson was wearing the face he had come to know as one with no fear, while gesturing to the inmates even though he was cuffed and bound.

"I'm Pittsburgh, I'm a Tender lion, yo ass is mine". He was hoping his charade had worked. He was hoping they would go back to their wards and let every body know that some crazy young boy was taken to the hole before he even got inside the gates. They had to know he had heart and no fear.

"Who in the f—was that crazy nigga" Jackson heard one of the inmates say. On the way to the hole, one of the guards asked "Why are you acting up Thomas, you haven't been here twenty minutes, what's your problem?" Jackson just looked as evil as he could without answering. He's going home to his family after a days work, Jackson thought. He's just doing his job; I've got to be here without a soul concerned with my well being. I've got to send a message to the prison population, that I am not a girl; a message that I will fight without provocation, without care of being hurt and with every intention of hurting someone else. He wanted to send a message before him, hoping someone recognizes his name and that he's not to be messed with. The door was slammed behind him. "Lock down cell c-15, no privileges for prisoner 3573 Thomas". He heard the lock click a second time to assure he would not be released when the rest of this tier was released for food and other inmate privileges.

Three times a day his food was slid under the door and remained there untouched until they came and took back the tray . . . for three days he went without eating and at times kicking his tray of food back out onto the tier, showing how stubborn he could be. On the fourth day a guard paused and spoke into the cell window saying, "Thomas, I don't care if you ever eat, but if you don't, they'll just take you to the infirmary and force feed you. Your gon'na be here a long time, sooner or later you'll eat". As he walked away, Jackson knew he was right. He pinched a piece of meat off of his food tray and ate it like a man tearing off flesh from his kill, uncaring about taste or what it was that was being eaten. He heard someone walking toward his cell to retrieve his tray. He pulled it in and began to eat what was left as quickly as he could. "Tray up", the outside voice said. He quickly dumped the remainder of his food onto the metal bed he had been sleeping upon and shoved the tray back under the door. He ate everything off of the bed and anxiously awaited the next meal. For sixteen days he stubbornly stayed in lock-down without conversation with anyone but God. Every cell had a bible, as if to say, this is your only source of help. He talked to God, and he talked to God, and then . . . he talked to God again. God never said a word . . . I the mean time his plan had worked; word was out that some crazy nigga named "Pittsburgh" was in confinement. During his final days in the hole things like cookies and cigarettes, even though he never smoked, were sneaked into his cell by inmates he knew while in Morganza. Notes were slipped in telling him to ask for one ward or another as his permanent quarters. He was finally released and sent to ward C which was the induction ward.

Chapter 12

Now there was a new cadence being called. "Step out, face your door, pull it up until it touches, when I say pull, close the doors; close them all at the same time, now pull!" All the doors were slammed hard at the same time, making a loud noise of metal cell doors slamming against their metal door jams and locking. Every time someone went into or came out of their cell the call was made, usually by the tier captain, (an inmate who was chosen after being on good behavior).

Jackson had yet to talk to anyone other than answering questions to the guards. Everyone on the tier was new and recently brought into Camp Hill. The connecting tier was made up of young men who were assigned to kitchen detail for the whole complex. White Hill was a city within its own walls. It had its own laundry, kitchen, tailor shop, barber shop, school system, furniture factory, farm area and many other work and training areas. Jackson heard a young man some where on the tier screaming to have his cell locked-down. He thought that it was probably to prevent the onslaught of a potential rapist or the threat of being beaten by a rival gang. In any system where all of the inmates are males, there is an unbelievable number of rapes and molestation. The average male reaches his sexual peak around sixteen years of age, that natural urge doesn't recognize where you are as a deterrent. For those born into these systems, rape is a sought after opportunity. It's not unusual that when a rape is being committed, many others standing by will participate after being caught up in the frenzy of sexual sounds and sights. The sexual frenzies make gang rape a commonplace. One way to not be victimized by these types of sexual abuses is to mate up with a harden prisoner or a husband and to become his property or, to fight your ass off until you are simply left alone. Jackson had never been raped nor did he ever experience a desire to rape another boy or girl. He did develop an instinctive dislike for bullies and rapist, even though they were often the males to fear in both Morganza and White Hill. He had yet to leave his cell for the first time when he began hearing more scuffling sounds of someone trying to survive. He was trying desperately to mind his own business. The screaming call for help echoed through his head. Though the sounds were far away, the voice sounded very familiar. Jackson couldn't stand it any longer. He stepped out of his cell and walked down one tier and onto the next. The cries for help were becoming louder as he got closer and closer to the source. Like so many times before Jackson's heart began to pound. He started to sense an on coming conflict. Three young men were standing approximately twenty feet in front of Jackson. One of the men turned and spotted him, not knowing if he was joining the effort or just walking on the tier. The face that was first to look Jackson's way with an all-to familiar evil grin, was that of the infamous Mohigan. He had also graduated to White Hill, and was working the kitchen detail. It was probably no coincidence that the kitchen detail was housed next to a ward that was set-aside for gays and temporary new comers. Mohigan either pretended or he actually didn't recognize Jackson. As Jackson cautiously approached, they began to stop prying the door and move away with words of promise to the cell occupant that they were going to get to him sooner or later. Jackson walked pass the cell still going toward the would-be rapist when a well recognized voice called out his name, "Jackie!" No one anywhere knew Jackson by the name Jackie other than people back in Coverdale. It was El-Tez. His eyes were wide open, he was absolutely jubilant.

"I'm so glad to see you, ah-man, I'm so glad to see you". He looked just as he did when Jackson had last seen him, only now he had a couple more missing front teeth and he was slightly reddened by the event of the bullies that were trying to enter his cell.

"I thought you were dead!" Jackson was just as glad to see his long lost friend. He thought El-Tez had died during the attempted escape at Morganza a couple of years before.

"Where have you been? How'd you get here?" They rattled questions back and forth to each other until lock-up time and Jackson had to return to his own tier. El-Tez told him that he had made it across the Morganza creek that night and that he waited and searched for him until he spotted search lights and was forced to go on without him. He caught a ride to Erie, PA, where he found some of his relatives and later went to Coatesville, PA. where he stayed with his mother until he was recently arrested for stealing a car and sent to White Hill. The body on the shoreline of the creek back at Morganza had been someone else's . . .

He had only been here for four days and had been doing everything in his power to keep those guys from running into his cell. He was badly beaten on his first night here, by Mohigan and forced to do something he would rather not talk about. The following day El-tez requested and received assignment to the cell next to Jackson's; from there they were later moved to K ward as permanent assignment. Jackson was assigned to the furniture factory and El-Tez was assigned to school. After work they each returned to K ward which housed a lot of boys and men from the Pittsburgh area. Having to fight was not as much of a concern at White Hill as it was at Morganza. The biggest fear here was being caught somewhere alone. After eight months of working in the furniture factory sanding chair legs by hand each and every day, Jackson was one of forty youths chosen to serve his time in forestry camp and luckily, so was El-Tez.

Chapter 13

The first campsite was located in a park called Pinchot and later moved to Pine Grove Furnace located at Caledonia State Park just northwest of Harrisburg. Jackson was assigned to cutting the first phase of a hiking trail that would later be extended all the way to Maryland and into West Virginia. They ate and slept in forty-foot mobile units that were strategically placed on the park grounds. Three trailers were sleeping quarters and one was a kitchen and dining, another was a recreation room and one was for restrooms and showers. One week-end of each month they were returned to the facility at Camp hill.

Starting in September 1963, they cut, removed and burned trees, shrubs and brush daily from 6:30 a.m. until 3:30 p.m. As they settled into their routine Jackson was chosen to run one of the two power chain saws. His job was to cut down trees, cut them into 4' pieces, while others cut off branches and stacked them for burning. Once the fires were burning, a prisoner was placed to watch each one until it burned itself out and then moved on to the next pile of wood. At the end of each day the fires were safely extinguished and they would head home singing and joking about all of these days' events and close calls. Unlike the main facility, the campsite became a bearable place to live and they quickly adapted to each other and to the guards. At fifty cents per day, Jackson was the highest paid prisoner of all of White Hill. The daily challenges of cutting down trees and plotting which way to go next; brought bonding and a sense of responsibility among the field crews. After each days work they devised sporting games like: field soccer and ice hockey. These games were roughly played and generally ended in a lot of pushing and shoving. Fighting would result in being shipped back to your cell-block at White Hill, which was enough of a threat to leave fighting alone. When there was an occasional fight, they were staged out of the guard's view and always a fair fight that ended with the recognition of the better man. Seldom did anyone get hurt. Rape was non-existing, though occasionally guys were caught performing sex acts that were usually over-looked. The winter was brutal and cold but they never lost a day of work due to the weather. They did loose the day of November 23, 1963, a day after the loss of our president. There was an indescribable sense of anger and confusion. There were clicks or groups of boys that spent most of their time together at work or play. Jackson's click discussed how they should be chosen to take-out who ever killed the president. They realized that the real criminals were at work. They, the great white suited people, had shown themselves by shooting the leader of our nation in the head. Any of youngsters would have given their life to be able to shove that killer's gun down his throat. This November day was filled with sadness. Jackson guessed that, in a way, they may all have felt guilty. They were all considered the bad guys of society. Does this mean that they were just like the killer? Is he one of us or are we, one of them? Are we capable of taking a life for financial gain or out of jealousy or racial hatred? Jackson didn't think so . . . most of these boys here at camp and back at White Hill were victims of circumstance. Motherless children unloved or misunderstood but there are just as many incapable of killing another human here at White Hill as there are on Capitol Hill.

Chapter 14

The forest fire in June . . .

Somewhere in Caledonia State Park there was a major fire. They were all called together and kindly asked by a state forest ranger to help fight a fire that was threatening homes and cabins just outside of the park's boundaries. Gladly, everyone that wasn't needed at camp volunteered to go and fight the forest fire. About thirty of them were loaded onto a bus. During the one-hour ride to the burning area we were given fire-fighting equipment and instructed on how to use the backpack. The pack had a container for water and a hand held spray nozzle for extinguishing small brush fires. We were instructed that when we reached the site of the fire some of us would be given digging tools. Those given digging tools would be given yellow vest and told to join a group of other volunteers to dig a six-foot firebreak on a ridge just east of the fire between the park and a small residential area. As we approached a clear field at the foot of the mountain, the burning area came into full view. 'Awesome', was the only word to describe the sight. Most of the mountainside to the left of them had been burned black with patches of trees still ablaze. The brush and treeless areas were smoldering and completely burnt out. The main fire appeared to be standing still with hot ashes billowing into the morning sky as far as his eyes could see. Jackson found himself hypnotized from the sight of such a large space being ravaged by this huge and seemingly slow moving fire. The smell of smoke filled the air as small whirlwinds had suddenly reached the bus area. As they got off the buses, other volunteers were lined up to get on. They were black with soot. Their eyes and mouths were the only distinguishable features on their faces. They were all dragging along exhausted and seemingly ready to fall down where they stood. This is real, Jackson thought, no show-off game. The fifteen in his group were carrying water back-packs and were directed to fill their tanks in the creek at the edge of the field and then to follow the troop leaders with a big black letter B on the back and front of their orange cover vest. Mr. Ritter, the guard in charge called Jackson to the side, "you're going to have to lead our boys, keep a head count of fifteen and don't take any chances. They keep calling our boys niggers and criminals, they've made it clear that they don't want us here. If I had my way we would be back on the bus and out'ta here". With that short speech he looked Jackson directly in the eyes and handed him a vest with a big B. "B group head out", came a command by a man dressed in military fatigues. "Get those busses out of here now"! Most of the busses were amidst the on-coming smoke and falling cold ashes. "Get'em-out'ta-here"! As Jackson looked at the busses now pulling off, he glanced once more at the leaving riders. They seemed to look sorry for Jackson and the new fire fighters. No one smiled or waved. There was just one look on every face and it was if as if someone had died. One smudged face looked at Jackson and gave a thumbs-up sign as the busses rolled out of sight. "Let's go! Let's kick some ass guys"!

They walked single file for at least an hour. About two hundred yards ahead Jackson could now see a line of men in an open area digging a fire stop with shovels and picks. The fire was no longer in sight. The bellows of smoke loomed just over the ridge in front of them.

"This is what we are going to do!" a forest ranger yelled. "We got'ta stop this fire from reaching the group of pine and evergreen trees just off to our right. Everyone with shovels and picks get in that line and help with the fire stop; for those with back-packs, the main fire is another twenty minute walk on the other side of the ridge. When we get there, space yourselves about ten feet apart, don't waste water, put your spray nozzles directly to the flaming ground grass and brush". He paused for a moment and listened to his hand held walkie-talkie. With a much more serious look, he told them to get busy and good luck. With his move a head gesture, they charged up the hillside wanting to join the fight like children playing army games. Reaching the top of the hill brought them to a whole new world of danger. The fire was roaring up the hillside about two hundred yards in front of them. To the left and to the right the flames were up to six feet high in the brush and just a foot off the grassy areas. They were first to reach the fire line burning down the hill. The flames moved slower coming up the hill and were now under foot, it seemed to pass right by the boys in a matter of minutes. Spraying and stomping as quickly as they could, they were able to slow down the line of fire directly in front of them; but in the rear where there were no men it quickly burned everything in its reach. They fought hard while slowly being backed up the hill by the flames. To their left the flames had gone another fifty yards and on their right and about four hundred yards away it had already reached the top of the hill. There were spots or patches of fire in several areas, but they had nearly stopped the fires progress in the center area of about two hundred yards. They had very little control over the fires on either side, now moving even faster with a wind which seemed to be coming up behind the fire out of the valley below. Jackson had run out of water and everyone else was out or spraying their last. They had failed to note which way to retreat to get refilled. Others had just begun to meet the fire line to our left. Jackson received instruction that a creek was about one-half mile back in the direction they had come. The crew was now running hard to the bottom creek for water. After refilling they returned to the center area where the flames had now re-kindled and were back into a full fiery force. The wind was now gusting and filled with hot ashes and smoke. As Jackson reached the flame line, the heat smacked him in the face, cinching his eyebrows. They pumped and sprayed trying to get back into control. They divided into two groups, while one group fought, the other headed for refills. After what seemed like eternity, they thought they were winning. The creek was now only about fifty yards behind them; they had been pushed back by the fire without realizing just how far. The fire seemed to be scattered to the left, it had already jumped the creek to our right. The blaze had forged right into the middle but it was still under control. They refilled our tanks again and headed towards the last burning area in sight. They proceeded toward the fire break, extinguishing burning areas along the way. They had started with a head count of fifteen, now they had twenty-two. After they completed the fire break, they started a back fire by extinguishing a fire along the break and causing the fire to burn itself out as the two burning areas met with unburned brush as fuel. It began to smolder and go out. As the main group of fire fighters came into view, we thought our efforts were to be applauded. "You idiots, you could have gotten killed in there. We told you assholes to clear the area an hour ago, you were the only idiots caught in the middle of the backfire"! Apparently, they had failed to give Jackson a walkie-talkie. They had no way of hearing the retreat call, so they stayed put and fought until the fire was out.

Experienced fire fighters were still arriving, although the fire was now contained to spotted areas. The valley and mountainside looked as if someone had torched it leaving nothing but the black ground and stumps. Behind Jackson stood the evergreen trees with camp sites and homes beyond, all untouched. They had held their own in spite of some bitching being done by some county sheriff. The sheriff asked everyone from White

Hill to line up, as they did, he began tying a rope around their waistlines, connecting each of them together. He began tying their hands with twine, when a man came forward and stopped him saying, "If they were going anywhere, they would have left already". He stopped but left the rope on our waist, instructing us to walk, one in front of another.

They got back to the pick-up area in about an hour, tired, exhausted and dehydrated. Jackson had never worked so hard in his life. He heard two sheriffs discussing what to do with them; saying they didn't want to be responsible. They instructed them to sit on the ground in a circle until a bus arrived to take them back to camp. Just beyond a line of fire trucks, they were feeding the fire fighters and passing out refreshments. Jackson's group had been instructed not to talk to anyone. So there they sat. It was nearly dark when they brought up a truck and turn the lights on them so they could remain in full view. One of the fire fighters finally brought them a water cooler and paper cups. They sat well into the night with head lights shining in their faces while waiting for the bus.

"What the hell is going on? Why are they hog-tied like this?" Mr. Ritter asked the sheriff. "These are trustees, they came to help and this is how you thank them"? "We didn't know what to do with them and I wasn't going to be responsible if they ran away"! "Take those damn ropes off and get on the bus". They were up and gladly got on the bus to some comfort. He went to the food area and brought back lunch bags of food and passed them onto the bus. I can't begin to tell you how good these single cheese sandwiches were. They all slept on the ride back to camp. Jackson never fought another forest fire, but he will always respect those who do. They deserve the gratitude; they are truly courageous

The summer days at Caledonia were a lot slower than those of winter. They were limited to an area where there was, no camping, hiking or other park activities. During these idle times, they were given the opportunity to prepare and test for a G.E.D. One of the trailers was set up and used as a classroom on weekday evenings. In about eight weeks of classroom studies, Jackson received his G.E.D. He had never done well in a classroom setting. Jackson's mind always seemed to wonder outside where life was actively being expressed.

As the winter began again to turn to spring at Caladonia State Park, the yearning for home returned day after day. The forestry work became routine and the campsite remained a safe haven. There are many stories to tell about life at White Hill and forestry camp. They would take a lot of writing and I'm sure this juvenile sector of Jackson's life must be becoming boring. I will summarize by saying that Mohigan was found dead just outside his cell window. Some say it was an attempt to escape other say it was the result of a set up by guards that were fed up with his abusive attitude. El-Tez was released about sixty days before Jackson. Most of the youth at forestry camp completed their G.E.D. requirements and learned enough at forestry camp to get a start at surviving on the street.

After serving more than two years Jackson was freed again and was given a go home suit and the two hundred and the fifty dollars that he had saved. He was sent home again.

PART TREE

Chapter 15

Home again; at age eighteen no longer cocky or proud but still young, strong and black. The new struggle was to find a job; hopefully one that paid more than sixty five dollars a week, which at the time was considered a decent pay for a young black guy. Also, to find a mate; the girl friend he had left behind lived in Clairton, Pennsylvania. She had written once a week when he had first arrived at White Hill and in his final year he received two letters one to say "she had a great summer vacation in New York" and another to say "I have been faithful and awaiting your return".

Upon his return needless to say he headed for Clairton to make his long awaited contact with his love. Jackson found himself with gonorrhea about four days later; so much for waiting faithfully for his return. He did quickly rebound and instantly fall in love with a girl name Sandy, a South High School senior cheerleader. She was truly a doll. They stayed close and as in love as two could be. He found a job in the J&L Steel mill. He purchased a 1958 midnight blue Pontiac and was well on his way to the rest of his life. He was bringing home more than eighty dollars per week, not bad looking and strongly attached to his new sweetheart. As the world turns life is not meant to roll along smoothly, it seems we must become predator or victim, but never that which is in between.

Before January of 1965 he was laid off by J&L Steel, his car needed a new transmission, his girl found a need for a new boy friend. He concluded that life was like the bumper cars at an amusement park. If you were to drive along in the bumper car and nothing hit you, the ride would ultimately become boring and uneventful. It's the collisions with others that make the ride a challenge. As you ride through life you can be broad sided, hit from the rear, the front or head on, by many different obstacles for many different reasons. That seems to be the way that life is designed. So you learn as he learned; to except the fact that you are going to be hit hard and let down many, many times. You are going to be hit from all angles and by everyone that comes near you. Some will do it viciously, some unknowingly. There will be those who hit you out of jealousy and contempt and those that may do it with good intentions. However you can bet your bottom dollar that it will be unending. So . . . brace yourself. Learn to avoid conflict when and if you can. You also need to learn when it's coming your way. Prepare for it, expect it, even look for it and maybe even cause it to happen. Jackson learned life's lessons long before his time. He could lash out at those who looked for trouble or he could easily bond to those that showed a need for compassion. Even so, he needed to find something to stand up and fight for. In June of 1965, with a little encouragement from the local law enforcement, Jackson left the Pittsburgh area, temporarily leaving behind his impregnated girlfriend. He headed for Washington D.C. His first choice was to join the military and onto the Vietnam War. He was turned down because of his juvenile record. His second choice was to fight racism. He quickly discovered that the opponent was very, very, wide spread. Though it was all around him by way of lack of employment, fair housing or affordable education, everyone confronted was in denial that it existed, yet . . . there were poor and jobless folks everywhere. The whites were, by comparison, employed, educated and well fed happy homeowners. Word in the white community had it that black folks are stupid, poor, lazy and if you live near one you become one. You do not turn black, so to speak, but you will become one by association and you certainly must be poor or foolishly stupid to want to live in the same neighborhood. Racism was one of many things that Jackson could not erase from his mind once he had discovered that it truly existed. All of his life he had kind-of felt sorry for them (white folks). They weren't very talented. They couldn't sing or dance very well. They didn't perform well at sports. They couldn't fight. They had no sense of humor, other than the stand up comedian, Red Skelton. In the institutions they were feminine and needed to be protected. He had heard that they all have small penises and focused mainly on oral sex. Their mommas' couldn't cook very well. Yet . . . yet they ruled the world and he didn't know why. Could it be that they have much better organizing skills. They march better. They shoot better. They hate better. They steal by making some theft legal. They cheat those who trust them. They climb to the top by stepping first on us and then on each other. They conquer. They are God's chosen. Why it's no wonder black folk don't have what they have as far as dollars, cars, education and homes. Actually, Jackson thought black folks were better off by far. Then he thought about the drug issue. Black folk being poor and happy seemed to irritate those who have everything. And those who are truly stupid turned to drugs and alcohol to pave a new way to utopia in hope of feeling like those who are powerful. We say; "this is what it must feel like to be in control of those at your feet."

In the inner-city, drugs seemed to be raining in from everywhere. For years it was only some white guy around the corner who supplied them and sometimes even gave them to attractive black females. They knew of no blacks that raised marijuana or were able to ship heroin or cocaine from the Orient or South America. Nor did they have pharmacist to supply us with so called 'legal drugs'. No way of manufacturing L.S.D. or other fabricated drugs in the communities then known as the ghettos. Some dictionaries say the word ghetto means, 'an inner city place where poor black folks live'. He thought, 'what a strange place to make money selling drugs'; among those who have the least. What a strange place to think that you'll become a successful drug dealer among those who own no businesses. In fact, it may be that it's the only place you can sell drugs and not be punished, then or now. Drug dealing did not become a serious crime until blacks began to benefit by the selling of drugs to their own for profit. Now, not only did they have ghettos, but now they had drug infested ghettos. Jackson had no interest in drugs, but he did have an interest in the equality that was being preached on the streets of Pittsburgh and all across the nation. He was interested in why there were so many racial issues in the streets of Watts, in La. Huff, in Cleveland, 14th St. in D.C. or the Hill District, in Pittsburgh and sections of other cities where hatred and disparity was overwhelming the black youths in our so called 'land of freedom and happiness'. These people were beginning to unknowingly become victims of genocide. These weren't Southern cities these were cities of freedom. Most cities were said to be over crowded with blacks. The need for manual labor was fast becoming a thing of the past. No war for white soldiers to fight. Vietnam was now just a place to send blacks and hope they would stay there knowing there was very little here to return to. No one seemed to remember why we were at war against Vietnam, even while the war was still going on. Many of his friends died there and those that made it back seemed displaced. Instead of war heroes they were just soldiers at battle saying things like, "we could win if we wanted to" but I don't think they were sure of just what it was they were suppose to win. Martin Luther King was often in the news leading the N.A.A.C.P. on non-violent marches. And the Peace Movement groups were continuously protesting against the Vietnamese war. The middle class white folks were now refusing to go to war. The upper class never went, and the blacks were lining up to go, as a way to escape jail and unemployment. Later, the singing group called The Temptations described it correctly in their song titled, Ball of Confusion, "that's what the world is today" saying "the only safe place to live is on an Indian reservation".

In Washington, D.C. the population was well over 75% black. Unlike Pittsburgh, black people there were working in banks, driving buses, owners of stores and new automobiles. Grocery stores and restaurants were filled with people of color. He had never seen so many black people. He didn't know such a world could exist. And yet, racism was just as prevalent in Washington as it was every where else.

A very close friend of his from Coverdale had moved to Washington, D.C. a couple of years earlier. He had joined the Metropolitan Police Department. Mack; had recently married a Washington sweet heart, named Shirley. They too had a newborn, in addition to a two-year-old son. They took Jackson in and introduced him to the city. He began to think that he was finally on the right track. Jackson married the mother of his first born but struggled to achieve compatibility. After seven months of marriage, cracks began to appear in his marital union. Jackson began to recognize a need of young black men to lock arms and unite against racism.

Jackson's young wife's calling was from a much higher source than his. His calling was to serve the black cause. Her calling was to serve God himself. The gap between the two of them grew rapidly. Before the end of July 1966, she had returned home three times to visit church and family and by late August she had left for an indefinite stay, taking their six month old daughter and the first love of his life with her. Jackson was fortunate enough to become employed by the Western Electric Company a subsidiary of AT&T at that time. He became what was called a long-lines switch board installer responsible for long distance services for the Nations Capital.

This is where Jackson met Freddie Morris, a strong civil rights activist from a Pennsylvania town about fifty miles south of Pittsburgh. Fred was a college student working his way through school as a switchboard installer. They were both assigned as part of a sixteen-man crew, installing long line operation switchboards for the White House area. Fred was very popular with the women and a very, very strong advocate of Marcus Garvey. At that time Jackson had never heard of Marcus Garvey or any of the other historical black heroes that Fred was so knowledgeable about. Back in Bethel Park historical heroes were all, and always, white males. History taught about famous British soldiers and early American Presidents, but never a black man, whether he be free or slave their were no black hero's present in his history book . . . period. On the other hand, Fred wasn't up to date on Jackson's recently found heroes like Angela Davis and H. Rap Brown. Jackson brought his own click to help him fight for the so called, 'cause'. In the early summer of 1966, he convinced the 409 members, Eddie

Brooks, El-Tez, Smittie Richardson and Bobby Lusha to move to D.C. and take up the fight against the pigs.

The Jewish Defense League and the Weathermen had both provided a spokesperson at one of the early rallies that Jackson had attended. For some unexplained reason Jackson connected to their cause and related it to the need of black youth to not fall asleep and let the same type of thing happen to blacks. After all, blacks have always been an easy target for those that wish to take from the helplessly poor. We are why some folks do any thing they can to move further and further away from the cities across the nation. It wasn't long before Jackson learned the meaning of racial hatred. He had no idea of how to hate, as those in the stories that were being told of how Jews were so hated, but he quickly began to feel the need to take up the cause as an act of bravery and to be willing to do what he had always done, that is, to come to the aid of the mistreated and abused. Jackson hadn't knowingly been subject to the type of racism that stood out as the hate of a race of people, he was more aware of the racism that prevented young blacks from an equal opportunity in the arena of recognized achievement and equal pay. The hatred of an individual because of his or her skin color, to him, seemed more ridiculous than any thing he could imagine.

Chapter 16

On August 25, 1966, Freddie Morris invited Jackson and his comrades of crime to attend a Marcus Garvey rally at Dupont Circle. The keynote speaker was a young man from the Student Non-Violent Coordinating Committee better know as SNCC, pronounced "Snick" his name was Stokely Carmichael. The rally was one of many that led to the famous protest at Cambridge Maryland; and the arrest of H. Rap Brown and a host of black local supporters. The rally introduced Jackson to the Panther Party movement and a part time Howard University teacher named Jimmy Gillesby. As SNCC supporters rallied to the non-violent call of their group, and the N.A.A.C.P. continued to rally for peace. Fred's group rallied for black education. Jackson's 'stand up and fight' minded inner circle began to rally for a new era of Panthers without a party. The small group of six named themselves the 409, New Era Panthers. They started off as a group of inner circle blacks, of ages between 18 and 25 with the adage that every one knew at that time, that 'we should trust no white man or black man over thirty.' The number one objective was to coordinate a group strong enough to make an impact on racism. Their approach was to take what they could from the establishment and generate as many dollars and weapons that it would take to get the attention of the racist government and to use every thing they could get to fight against the KKK's white power movement that was in the process of arming what was thought to be a growing Southern Militia.

The Militia was supported by the National Rifle Association and according to the 409' s beliefs, they were being recruited by every police department in America. In their minds white Americans were involved in a plot to send blacks into Vietnam or back to Africa and those who refused would be placed in penal institution across the country via the blessing of J. Edgar Hoover; who they were convinced, closed his eyes while president Kennedy was assassinated; because of his views on equality. White American males were constantly bombarding their women and children with the notion that "black men were bad, not all of them of course, but the majority of blacks are lazy thieves that would like nothing better than to take away the white way of living", of course most black males were only concerned about food, clothing, shelter, a car and a girl to love. The thought of disrupting the lives of white people was and always will be a notion that is strictly for those who are wasting their lives in stupidity. It is hard enough for an enslaved man to achieve respect by defending his rights by any means available, it would only lessen his hope of growing stronger if he were to focus on why he can not achieve the same status of respect of his captors without revealing the fruitlessness of envy and the vain desire to destroy a less spirited race of people.

Jackson, like many other young blacks, had his sights on bringing Black Power to the inner cities based upon pride of ownership and the courage to wage war against racist and predatory conditions, this did not include a war against any family or individual. The plan was to show 'whitey' that blacks could be just like them when it came to forcing a change for the betterment of the country and all of it's people. And just like them, it was determined that to stand up and fight is the only language that is understood all over the world. While the primary group of Panthers from La. stood up for their rights and got most of the attention. The underground movement began to spread rapidly throughout Washington and into Baltimore, Philly, Newark, and Chicago. In Chicago the Black Stone Rangers had already built a foundation for a black supported attitude that would "take no Shit." The movement then connected to black cities across the nation, from the Black Panther Party to black power; from a Black Panther attitude, to black pride. This may seem far-fetched and slightly crazy now, but in 1966 it was a realistic and a necessary effort. They were truly convinced that most white people were full of hate and set on ridding their nation of Black Americans by ways previously mentioned.

The Nation of Islam had been continuously bombarding the inner city with "hate whitey" messages. Seemingly on every corner "Mohammed Speaks" literature was being sold to communities already confused about why God favored the white race, ignored the yellow race and continuously punished the black race. Yet, Mohammed was preaching that Allah was truly black and that the devil was a white man in a police uniform.

Back in Pittsburgh, Jackson's wife was convinced that the end of the world was just days away. Jehovah Witnesses absolutely knew that the world, as we knew it, would end within the next few years.

As a group of young black men bent on surviving the whites and . . . the wrath of God, they forged a bond and committed to a brotherhood of black power. Black women all over the country had spearheaded the cause by urging men to stand up and fight for their rights. The feeling of love began to spread through the communities. Black folk recognized each other with gestures of respect and by black power signs that quickly caught on as an acknowledgment of a brotherhood.

On the West Coast, Hewey Newton had sent a message demanding equal rights and the right to bear arms. Police intimidation was rampant all over the country. Even inner city black policemen knew that exercising any freedom of speech to a pig was intolerable. A pig was the respected title given to white policemen because of their common piggish posture of being big, fat and carrying a big stick on the city streets.

The white people of compassion were labeled nigger lovers and held in check by the threat that their children would be sent to Vietnam or arrested for obstruction of justice. It was truly a code that no one interfered with the arrest or beating of a black man, especially a young so-called troublemaker that may have been tempted to asked why a man could be thrown to the ground, searched and beaten.

Jackson couldn't understand racism. He was raised in a predominately white community composed of immigrant coal miners. His community was considered poor and after a hard days work in the mines everyone was black. The only things that were white were the teeth and the warm smile of people that did not recognize color as a barrier. Or, the fear that could be seen in the whites of the eyes of those who may have had love ones trapped a mile or more below surface in a collapsed mine. These were people of the American blue-collar workforce. Folk who didn't really want racism. These were people who believed in, 'live and let live'. These were small villagers from Europe and blacks that were imported from down south that had found their way to the north for the purpose of working for a living.

One true observation of the beast or god of racism is that just like the other gods of doom and evil, most people don't recognize the beast until it affects their own lives and when they do the general response is, "better you than me." It seems unfitting that the Holy Bible recognizes it's beast of jealousy, adultery and such, while the beast of racism lies well hidden and comfortable in the hearts of the most righteous of men.

The Black Power Movement was not against white folks because of their skin color, color of their eyes, or their straight hair; it was about their unwillingness to defend the rights of all people that dwell in this so called world melting pot. Actually, the movement wasn't against people of any color. In Jackson's group it was about their desire to be recognized and respected as men. It was to establish a base in preparation for defending themselves against the aggression and abuse of the racist.

They felt destined to initiate change. The so-called establishment must begin to acknowledge their existence and back off rather than plan to exterminate blacks. Jackson's group had all but abandoned religion. This was not about God, to them this was about respect for life and keeping it at all cost.

On August 26, 1966, two groups, The Weathermen and the J.D.L, assisted Jackson in spearheading about thirty young black men that he had known from his juvenile days, mostly from the Philadelphia, Newark and different parts of Washington, D.C. They met at Haines Point Park to choose five leaders for the New Era 409. Under the disguise of having picnics, they spent the whole day planning ways to communicate by phone and on the streets with black power signs of brotherhood. One of the weathermen's spokespersons opened Jackson's eyes to many issues pertaining to how our Government was being ran and how the primary focus was to keep poor people poor and filled with God, while they forged ahead owning every thing of value in the here and now. He brought to Jackson's attention that the powers of the government were running wild with the notion that white supremacy was not only a natural phenomena, but one that needed to occur in order to attain a safe environment for all of the white people of America. The only way to achieve the goals of the racist was to demeaned and intimidate the black man just as John Lynch had suggested back in the days of slavery. The question to Jackson was "what are you people going to do, lay down like cowards or stand up and fight for your rights?" Jackson had no answer nor could he relate to how fighting our own countrymen could lead to a resolution pertaining to the hardships that black people were facing. He had believed that the short comings of the black man was do to the excuses that he and others like him had always been taught; that 'Blacks need more education, more family and Bible orientation, more skills and craftsmanship, more this or of that. It hadn't dawn on him that blacks had what it took and were very viable in every phase of life other than acceptance. They urged him on, "come on Jackson wake up your people need you. They are waiting for your people to stop being sleeping giants. Get up and do something. They hate you people more than any other race on earth because you won't fight for yourselves. You just wait around like passive sheep for something to be done for you. If not now, when, when will you standup."

Jackson was starting to become offended by mankinds on slot of accusations that blacks were simply cowards. Of course we're afraid, he thought, anyone would be afraid. The thought of going to prison is a tormenting thought. The fear of being taken away from the small bit of freedom that we've come to know is is an overwhelming feeling. Especially when you've been embedded with the thought that, we should appreciate what we have and be thankful to God for all the good things that He has given us. "Why is it that you people will kill a man for stepping on your shoes at a party? but say nothing when a white man steps all over your rights. Come on . . . do something . . . the world is waiting for you people to demand justice and all you do is talk."

"I do more than talk" Jackson said in a knee-jerk response to the mans insults. "We do a lot."

"So I guess that's why your people always make the least amount of money. That's why the jails are crowded with your color. That's why you have kissed their ass for the worst of jobs. That why you people live in the slums. Are you fighting to stay in the projects or to wait in line for a welfare check to feed your family? Is that your fight? Are you fighting or even wondering why the majority of you will never be more than third class citizens. Doesn't it bother you that you've been classified as being three-fifths of a man even at your best? Come on, what is wrong with you people, what will it take to wake you up and do what ever it takes to be counted?" Jackson was angry, not so much about what was said, he was angry because it was all much to close to being the truth and he couldn't begin to comprehend what he or any other black man could do about it.

"We'll be talking to you Jackson, in the mean time, think about what we said. Let it digest and let us know when your ready to do your part, you and your black Kittens . . . oh . . . I meant to say black panthers." With that last remark hitting Jackson personally he responded by angrily saying, "Okay lets not go so far with the insults that it causes you to get your asses kick."

"That's the spirit" the man said, "get angry enough to kick the asses of those that hate you, not us, we're on your side. We'll be seeing you."

Jimmie Gillesby was elected as our terminal of communications. Jackson was selected to develop ways for the funding of arms and food. He knew why he was chosen and realized the importance of his position. He surrounded himself with people he trusted and could count upon. He chose his own. Those with brave hearts and willing to die for our cause. He had El-Tez out of Philly, Eddie Brooks his homeboy, Bobby Lusha from South Philly, Jimmy Bodean of Newark, and Smittie Richardson of Baltimore. They made a pack to be willing to die for each other and to never give in to the white man's domination. They didn't shake on it or stack hands or share blood. They did it with a look. A quick glance at one another that said, its our turn to show the world that we are warriors. They aligned with others from Washington D.C. and begun a new movement in support of the Black Panthers of La. and the Black Power movements all over the country. Within weeks Bobby began to recruit men and women who could connect to the cause. All new recruits were made to believe this was a social group. With the financial help of the white underground they sponsored picnics, parties, drag races and sporting events every weekend in an effort to identify the stronger more dependable people. They encouraged members to move into Southeast Washington, which had become a stronghold for young blacks from all over the East Coast and especially the Pittsburgh area.

August 28, 1966 while looking for a group of men from Uniontown, Pa., that lived on Ainger Place in Southeast Washington and having an incorrect street number, Jackson knocked on an apartment door belonging to a group of young black girls from Midland, Pa. Of which one of them was Gloria. The mother of Jackson's daughter was out of his life and had grown away from him and onto her pursuit of religion. She had left him and his dedication to the cause, far behind. He had briefly forgotten his natural attraction to the opposite sex until knocking on that wrong door.

She was about 5'9" with a smooth youthful brown complexion. Very thin from her shoulders to her waist line and stunningly shapely from her waist to her ankles. Her legs were visually soft as pearls, her eyes sparkled with innocence, and her lips were always moist and naturally parted just enough to see the bottom of her upper teeth. After being introduced he was told that she was involved with a man named Larry who hadn't arrived to pick her up for an expected date. Jackson instantly hungered to hug the young girl from Midland. He couldn't take his eyes off of her as she sat talking and smiling each time their eyes met. She was wearing a very revealing mini skirt that was causing her some discomfort because of his constant staring at her legs. She was obviously shy and wasn't aware of her own attractiveness. She was here in Washington to start her career as a government employee. Surrounded by her life long friends, she appeared excited and happy to be alive and that, she was. As the time came for Jackson to leave, he took one more glance hoping to confirm any interest she may have. She kindly said goodnight without any indication or connection. When the door closed behind him, he wanted to run back in and tell her 'I love you' or maybe just to catch one more glimpsed. As they exited the building two guys were entering Jackson assumed one of them was her date. Needless to say, he was slightly jealous and afraid he may never see her again, just as the girl of his dreams back at Morganza.

Chapter 17

That next morning was one that he was very glad to see. He was awakened by a phone call from Fred. They were to have a meeting at the home of a man who was hosting a group of people from Chicago and after the meeting Jackson insisted that they have a party at his apartment. He made sure the girls from Midland were invited and that most of the crowd would be their own associates from the Pittsburgh area.

By 9:00 p.m., his apartment was packed with people dancing, drinking and eating everything in sight. It was his way of getting away from the seriousness of life and to hopefully get to lay his eyes on the girl from Midland.

At about 11:00 p.m. they came; Gloria and two other girls from Midland, Pa. She was fresh, dressed in a miniskirt and all legs. They began dancing the minute they got inside. Jackson wasn't much of a dancer, but he enjoyed watching her dance. On every song she was on the floor smiling and making all the faces that dancer make while enjoying the soulful beat of groups like the Temptations. Jackson waited patiently for a slow song, so he might get to her and ask for a dance and hold her close. At the beginning of every song he imagined that she looked his way, as if to say "come dance with me." But he didn't know how to do the latest dances nor did he want to embarrass himself by letting her and others know. Finally a slow song started, as he hesitated to make sure it was a slow song, someone approached and asked her to dance before he could reach her. Jackson could see that she was clearly disappointed that he hadn't got to her first. She kept her eyes on him as she responded to a slow grinding body contact of her dance mate. As the night went on he couldn't seem to get that long awaited slow drag. The dance style was to grind as hard as you wanted and the females accepted it. This body contact was what every guy awaited. Jackson just wanted to touch her but wasn't having any luck over the guys who were fast dancers and never giving her a chance to sit down.

The song started, Jackson made his move and was at her side and grabbed her hand just after someone else grabbed the other and asked her to dance. She said, "he asked me first" gesturing at Jackson. Finally, Jackson awkwardly pulled her to him with his left-hand holding her right and his right hand wrapped around her waist; she gently put her left arm upon his shoulder. He was in heaven. She felt so good. She smelled so fresh this was so right. He wanted to hold her close and grind like others she had danced with; but he didn't have the rhythm. He didn't want to make her think he was just another presumptuous nigga.

She pulled her right hand out of his and placed it around his neck and then gently pulled herself against his body. Jackson thought he was on the verge of orgasm as she placed her head to his chest with her lips facing his but not quite touching. He didn't want the song to end. Other guys were just waiting to be next to dance with her. As the record began to end he squeezed himself against her as hard as he could. When the music stopped he refused to let her go. He stood holding her for what seemed like an eternity, without music, without words. She stood there with him as if they were alone and belonged to each other. The music started again and though it was a fast song she stayed close, as if she did not want to let go. She began to move to the up beat of the music but Jackson was lost. Rather than stumble around he let go, turned and went out the door and out onto the entryway to savor his moment alone. As he looked back the next waiting guy was surely bopping his way in front of her for a dance. He sat on the steps outside thinking that she was inside dancing with someone else when suddenly she sat down beside him.

"It's crowded in there," she shyly said.

"I know, I had to get some air. It's so pretty out tonight would you like to go for a ride?" he boldly ask.

"Yea, I would like that," she said, to his surprise and much to his satisfaction.

With the party still going on they got into his convertible Pontiac and rode off listening to music and talking about nothing and everything. He just knew he was in love with this girl.

'Should I tell her I'm married with a child and one on the way. Oh no, she may walk away. He didn't want to take the chance of losing what he'd finally found. What should I tell her? Where should I take her? Can I keep her? What will she think if I lie? Just shut up and enjoy her company. That was his final decision. 'If she's gone tomorrow I will have this night to remember.' Every time she looked away, he looked at her. He thought she was a jewel. After their ride they returned to the party which was just about to end. Before going back inside she paused and stood directly in front of him. He pulled her close for the hug that he had craved for all night long. Without a word, she held still as he squeezed her as tightly as he could. As Jackson began to release her she placed her lips against his and kissed him; sloppy and sweet were her lips. She quickly turned and entered the door "thank you" she said "for the ride . . . and the kiss".

Chapter 18

One of the girls in his group that was employed by Armor Security Company, informed them of several job openings for night security guards. She was in charge of scheduling and assigning locations. Initially, we hadn't realized the potential of having our own people in such low paying jobs, until someone suggested the possibility of ways it may benefit the cause.

The network between Washington, Newark, and Philadelphia was rapidly developing. At the top of the needs list was food, clothing, guns and of course money. The Black Panther Party had established what is now known as Food Banks and Kitchens for Children, as part of the self-sustaining effort for creating pride in our communities. The 'Need to Feed' was the number one call. Food stamps had just began to reach black communities and most stores still hesitated to accept them. In some ghetto areas around Chicago and Gary, Indiana folks couldn't get enough food to last through the month. Hunger was quickly becoming a priority over education. The call was out for food. The means of delivery had been organized well enough to fill the vehicles that were voluntarily transporting goods.

Our newly established network succeeded only in recognizing the needs not the means. Word on the street had it that the food taken in the Detroit riots had been depleted. Young blacks were uprising in every city in America. Most of them wanted to step up and do something. In the inner cities the nights belonged to the blacks. Through music, grapevines and house to house gossip the word had spread that blacks must rise up and protect ourselves, feed themselves, demand equal rights and equal education.

One of the first tips from the Weathermen, was the Washington Redskin's football stadium. Six guards were assigned nightly to play watch dog over the empty stadium between games and daytime business activity. Jackson and a brother named Curt were the only two assigned from the hood. The other four were regulars with full time guard jobs. They apparently were filling in for guards who had gone on vacation.

It wasn't long before Jackson's comrades and a slew of new young blacks from all over the east coast began to secretly gather in the Nations Capital to clear up the misconception that all black men were spineless and accepting of what ever was being dished out to them. The peace marches had become fruitless and nauseating to the young blacks that had watched and listen to the likes of Huey Newton, Angela Davis, Fred Hampton, Stokely Carmichael and H. Rap Brown, to name a few, They began to stand up and see that Martin Luther King, like all of the other world wide known non-violent leaders, marched for cause after cause only to win second or third class citizenship.

Europeans got what they wanted and ruled the world with wars and rumors of wars. Churchill did not stage a non-violent protest against Hitler. The United States did not respond to Japan with chants and peace signs. Kennedy did not ask the Soviet Union to 'stay out of Cuba or we will stage a friendly protest march'. We are in America; here they combat wrong doings with a fight back or die attitude, not the 'we shall overcome through God' or the begging for fairness and equality. This was not their way of doing things, it was more of a, 'do as we say do, not as we do', to voice your disapproval of a racist country such as ours. Of all the many immigrants and refugees that fled their countries to get to America over the years, we were the only nationality that strived and yearned to go back to our own country. We were enslaved and brought here by force and never welcomed.

Jackson's comrades did not become a part of the Black Panthers as they were publicly known in La. and other cities. They became a new and formidable group of elite young angry black men that dubbed themselves as a new and different group of Panthers, a new era, 'the 409'. They didn't wear the popular black leather jackets or sleek black gloves that had became a symbol of defiance. They kept the low profile of young men that were up to no good, even though the cause was justified. There was a questionably thin line between whether they were politically minded Black Panthers or, as F.B.I director Hoover put it, "common criminals and a threat to society". They were bent on survival and saw nothing wrong with taking what ever they could from the white establishment when and where ever they could. Jackson was quick to become the ring leader and a key organizer of their own movement to gain respect and fortune for himself and his people. A movement that would not hesitate to use non-violent crimes against an enemy that seemed to have everything while they had nothing. The inner circle members were as straight as one could be during the day and waited for every opportunity to strike the establishment from Washington to Western Pennsylvania on any given night.

The Jewish holocausts, which was a merciless mass murder of millions of Jewish men women and children by the dominating German Government, was an example of how deep the hatred of a race or religion can run, and, just how ruthless it can be when men blindly follow their leaders. The rage in the one heart of the huge mind of many men had set itself out to destroy the very roots of happiness or to "leave no stone unturned". They struck their hardest while the victims were on their knees in prayer to personally squeeze God from the hearts of a people that were chosen. The voices of hatred still go on to this day and of all the races or religions that have ever existed, none have lost more lives, none have been more hated than those with darkened skin. Ironically, they are the most forgiving, and the most pure at heart. The killing of masses of people is obviously not as pleasurable while the would-be foe is standing tall.

During the declared war of the 409, they respectfully received a tip that the National Rifle Association had a shipment of advanced weapons at the D.C. stadium to be put on display and later sold to their members, "for the protection of their love ones against the black criminal aliments that had infested the streets of the inner cities across America." Later, the 409 learned how the police department manage to enlist so many white deputies during the declaration of a state of emergency in order to clear the streets during civil disturbances, the 409 suspected that the same racist that bought the advanced weapons from N.R.A. were the same recruited members (mostly KKK) appointed deputies during any inner city disturbance. Thanks to the Weathermen's tip Jackson and his clan was able to intercept the weapons shipment and relieve the Nation Rifle Association of nearly all of their goods. Within days they dispersed the weapons to Chicago and to the west coast for the cause. Not a cause that would use the weapons to go on the offensive but the cause that would defend if necessary.

With the tips that were given they took out the Giant food store warehouse and other big businesses establishments that were suppliers and distributors of any goods that they could sell or contribute. They respectfully relieved the Giant food store chain of tons of food for the needy in Washington, Philadelphia and Newark. They invented the crash and grab from bared windowed liquor stores for goods to be sold on the streets. They, so called 'knocked off' establishment after establishment under the orchestration of Jackson to get ahead in a land of opportunity where the only opportunity for a young black man was to take what he could from those who have more than they could have possibly earned, and to do it without being caught. They, indeed, were finally doing well, both financially and emotionally. They were winning, in their own way, a war that the enemy didn't even know was going on. They were likened to an ant stealing bits of food at the city dump. No battle to be won. The giant was not about to fall. Jackson's group was no more than a group of niggas stealing and expecting to screw a racist nation, when in reality they could only screw up and eventually get caught and thrown into jail with the rest of the so called revolutionaries. The 409 was at war only in their own minds. The white racist mechanism was too big to notice Martin Luther King's noises or the Panther's balled fisted war efforts or the Muslims hate whitey campaign as being anything but a statistical annoyance.

Chapter 19

A drizzling rain was falling on Washington D.C. most of the day. Occasionally he could hear sudden down-pours of rain beating against the windows. This was the day that began to awaken and momentarily unite a frustrated race of people.

It was April 4, 1968. Most of our inner circle activist lived in or near an apartment complex called Barnaby Terrace. The buildings were constructed of poured concrete walls and entry ways. It was virtually a fortress against any aggressive gun fire. Directly across the street was an open field, a few one story structures and a post office, all easy targets from the windows of Barnaby Terrace if such an attack were to occur. Southern Avenue was the boundary between Maryland and Washington D.C. To the rear side were concrete walled patio doors and a high-rise view of old S.E. Washington apartment complexes that were filled with thousands of black families who were living in poverty without knowing it. There was a parking lot that acted as a barrier between the older units and the newly built units that Jackson's group occupied. The young black occupants had planned many ways of egress from building to building through an upper attic crawl spaces that led from one section to another and ultimately to the lower floor patio doors that exited all over the building. Within five miles of Barnaby Terrace, there were similar apartment complexes that housed different sectors of the New Era black power movement.

Many nights of meetings resulted in a plan of defense that would protect the thousands of blacks that lived within the perimeters of occupied apartment strongholds. They intended to fight if and when the whites attempted to eliminate blacks via the neighboring state of

Maryland. They were convinced that the termination would begin while many of the young blacks were in Vietnam or while they were killing off each other in street violence. Reports of police brutality and killings were being passed through the neighborhood grapevine daily. The rumors of summer riots were often confirmed by inner city news reports of blacks being murdered during traffic stops and lynching throughout the south. Blacks occasionally retaliated by burning and looting white owned businesses, thinking this would show that blacks had the courage to fight back. They were learning to first, recognize the enemies, who they were and how they intended to break the spirits of young black men. The enemy list included the police, or pigs, rollers, the man, red-necks, or any street name used to describe the number one enemies, mainly the police forces of America. There was a warning call whenever two or more blacks gathered. They really thought that policemen were the army used against them. The so-called "protectors", were assigned to protect only the whites from blacks and Jews. Jewish people understood their troubles and often stood up on behalf of blacks, knowing that they would be next. Blacks were hated because they were black. Jackson had no idea why whites hated Jews, especially white Jews. He had thought that it was a black thing.

Within one mile from Barnaby Terrace there were six liquor stores; just as most of Washington's inner city communities, S.E. blacks were well supplied with drugs, alcohol and outdated guns. The means to self-destruct were in place. Blacks were economically confined to certain areas by what they called the invisible fence, (the obstacles placed between white communities and the black and poor communities). Police were sent in nightly to show white dominance and supremacy without mercy. Companies were apparently willing to sacrifice businesses that were located within the ghetto zones in exchange for new structures now beginning to be built in suburban industrial areas; even to the point of burning there own businesses during black turmoil and blaming it on so-called 'rioting'.

On the day that King was shot, before the news reached television and radio broadcasting, the word had been out on the streets that Martin Luther King had been assassinated in Memphis, Tennessee. Jackson received his call from Freddie Morris. "Brother", he said, "did you hear what happened to King"?

"No", Jackson replied.

"He was shot to death in Memphis".

"Oh No" Jackson felt his old friends fear and anger weakening the very legs he stood upon. "If they've killed him, heaven only knows what they'll do to us, he was a good guy. What are we going to do?" Jackson asked.

"Brother, let's sound the call to arms!" Fred responded.

The Klu Klux Klan was the most notorious non governmental organization of the time; thought to be under the leadership of Director Hoover of the FBI. Blacks were aware of the oath they had taken to destroy so called "niggers in America". They were assumed to be responsible for the King assassination. The call to arms meant to fight to our death, not to lie down and die or be hung from a tree. For the black race a call to arms was more mythical than real.

Twenty-eight young men belonging to the D.C. black power movement by way of the 409 were residents of Barnaby Terrace, including Eddie Brooks, El-Tez, and Jim Bolden, and Curt Toler. They lived in or near Jackson's two bedroom unit. They armed themselves and met in the rain at the parking area on the northern side of the complex. One after another they showed up, heads hung in sadness; standing, sitting and leaning against cars. Quietly they came together in anticipation of what was about to happen next. "What we gon'na do Jackson? They've killed King and we don't know who else; all we do is talk, what-chew gon'na do Jackson?" the young man repeated. Jackson had no answer. They continued to stand in the rain waiting for everyone to show.

With nothing but the sound of rain, they stood soaked to the bone, confused and in need of leadership. Jackson assumed Fred was a leader, Fred assumed Jimmy was the leader. The more violent and criminal minded men, looked to Jackson for leadership, while others assumed leadership would come from Muslims or the Panther Party. Some thought the only real leader had been murdered when King was shot. Jackson's realization that violence has no leader was fast becoming a factor in this long feared moment of truth. A leader of violence, even with a cause, must be relentless. Martin Luther King may have been right in a lot of ways but if their only hope is to dream and they could not forcibly pursue it, it will always be just a dream. Force can be applied in a lot of ways. Jackson knew his blacks didn't have the heart to retaliate recklessly and risk harming innocent whites; that would be far worse than racism. He couldn't lead random acts that may harm innocent people. "What are we gon'na do?" came again from the same voice that had earlier broke the silence. This voice was from a member who was a known killer; who had no love for anyone white or black, he and many like him were filled with hate and to him now was a time for vengeance. Now was a time to kill someone, anyone, just to vent personal frustration, perhaps like the shooter of Martin Luther King. Jackson wasn't sure there was an organized plot against blacks as a people. He also knew most of his comrades were not killers. They had a shallow minded plan to protect themselves not to attack anyone. They never really thought that such a time would come. The thought was that other whites would not allow the slaughter of black people

He wondered about the safety of his family back in Pittsburgh, including his two daughters. He wondered how many blacks were being killed as they stood there helplessly in the rain. Could we really defend ourselves or anyone else? Where do we start? Where is our enemy?

In the background of their silence they could hear the many police and fire sirens. The group had now grown to about sixty men and a few women. Even with the numbers growing they still remained relatively silent. Many had started to pace and walk from small group to group talking quietly. Most were angry but all wore that frightful look of concern. Jackson instinctively knew where leadership comes from. He also knew that when instinct is overcome with rage, humans do stupid things. When instinct is overcome by desperation, humans do stupid things. When instinct is led by misinformation, it results in confusion. When instincts are led by compassion, it creates leadership. Leaders are born from a love for people. Jesus was a leader, He ultimately brought hope to the races with the strength of his miracles, not the power of his words. Martin Luther King was a leader, he died while preaching against racism. His strength was in the prophecies of his dreams and the belief and hope that things were going to change very soon. He performed no miracles other than the ability to bring black folk together. Whoever leads under circumstances of rage, desperation and confusion becomes a person leading a mass of blind followers. He becomes a part of a being made up of a crowd. This mass of people will be willing to swallow-up anything in its path without thinking; similar to, as the saying goes, a bull in a china shop, unknowing or caring about what damage that is done Jackson's instincts led him to close ranks in the rain soaked parking lot of Barnaby Terrace. "Everyone, listen." He said in a calm and gentle voice. "Fred is not coming here tonight. He is with our brothers at Stanton Road hopefully planning their next step. Tomorrow morning we will meet at seventh and Florida Avenues N.W. Spread the word. Tonight we mourn; tomorrow we will find our enemy and fight." Remembering a fist fight he once won, he said, "Tomorrow we tuck in our bottom lip, close our eyes tightly and swing, maybe with God's help we'll hit something. Go home and cry"

"They killed an innocent man!" someone shouted as everyone began to humbly walk away and wait for tomorrow.

This night's decision didn't please Jimmy who was a member of his own imaginary death squad. He wanted to use this occasion to strike. He was one of the elite who had been asked to take up arms and speak the only language white folk understand and respect. Take up arms and fight for your rights. Fight for your African rights. He had killed in Vietnam and wouldn't hesitate to kill again but who would we kill? Jackson still could not identify the aggressor. The enemy was every white man but not some white men; certainly not white women and children. The enemy was some policemen; but not all. Who was the K.K.K.? Who was the FBI? Where was the uncle Toms? Give us this beast named racism so that we may put a bullet in its head. Our enemy was evasive, cunning, relentless, cold-blooded and yet righteous. He was everywhere and nowhere. Many nights as a teen in Morganza Jackson cried himself to sleep wishing he were home. Now again, he found himself as a twenty-two year old black man wanting to cry. He is not an ordinary black man. He is a strong and foolishly brave black man. One with compassion, as well a cunning sense of survival, yet at this time he felt that they would all be dead or in prison within weeks. He knew this was the beginning of an end.

Jackson went inside and called his mother, speaking to her for the first time in more than a year. "Momma," he said, "Take care of the family. I hope we all live through this".

His mother responded and said, "It's a shame they killed that NAACP man, he was a good man just like Adam Clayton Powell. I feel so sorry for his wife and kids . . . what are you talking about? Live through what?" she asked, "You think they'll catch the man who did it? I hope he's not a black man."

"Momma, this is it, we're gon'na stand up and fight," Jackson said.

"Boy, don't you be no fool, you're always in the middle of things that don't concern you, let the police handle it. They'll get'm and God will punish him. You need to take care of your kids and stop get'n into trouble!" She was in a different world Jackson thought.

"Ma, we can't just sit by and let this stuff continue to happen."

"You just stay out of trouble," she said, "I don't want to see you in jail son, let somebody else do it".

"Bye Ma, tell everybody I called."

"Goodbye, remember what I said, stay out of it!" with that, she hung up.

Jackson forgot or didn't know how to say I love you and nor did she. He thought that the long time feared race war had started and that they may never see each other again. She thought it was just another racist killing.

Later, as the damp and dreary night fell upon South East Washington D.C., Jackson and his closest young black militant comrades stood looking off of a forth floor balcony at the apartment complex. To their right, the view of Saint Barnabus Road resembled a scene of a city under siege. Most of the small businesses were ablaze. Sirens were wailing off into the distance in every direction. The horizon was filled with billowing smoke and flickering flames engulfing entire buildings. It had been raining since early that morning and now the particles of burnt ash had mixed with the drizzling rain causing nightfall to come early. To their left at about two hundred yards, two to three hundred people were on the streets looting and moving in and out of every structure that hadn't been set afire. The obvious but questionable observation was that there were no police cars, fire trucks or any other vehicles of authority in the entire Southeast sector. These men knew why. Less than an hour before, the local five o'clock news declared that Martin Luther King Jr. had been shot to death in Memphis Tennessee. The call to arms had been sounded in many of the inner cities across the country. These young militants considered this shooting as a signal that what had been predicted was finally upon them. Now, they were not alone in the raising of their fists. Now, there was a loud and clear message to the conservatives of the so-called 'peaceful route to equality'. The man of peace, the man of tolerance, a man of God, had been shot down like a common enemy of a foreign nation. This was truly the last straw. In the minds of these six proud young men and many like them, this was the start of war. What was on the minds of the looters, only God knew.

The communications between the thirty or so groups of New Era Panthers known in the Washington D.C. area was very lacking. There had been many back door meetings, rallies and support protests, but nothing had actually been planned to encounter anything of this magnitude. There was certainly no plan of how they might survive an all-out assault from the racist mechanism that had been in place for more than two hundred years.

The 409, whether they wanted to be or not, was now a part of an elite group that was not affiliated with the National Black Panther Party. Though they had no workable plan of defense against any enemy, there was a plan pertaining to where to meet and rally against issues that had always confronted the masses of blacks in the Washington area. That meeting place was Florida Avenue N.W.

The next morning they headed out . . . Like the forest fires of Caledonia, the smoke hung heavily over the nation's capital. Instead of trees aflame, it was the homes and businesses of those representing the power of white dominance. They drove as a part of a caravan of cars, heading for Florida Ave. destination. The word had spread quickly and much broader than they had anticipated. Upon arrival, expecting a hundred or so members, they found thousands of people waiting to participate in what ever was going down. Amazingly, there was a sense of calm, even though the sounds of sirens and the sight of burning buildings loomed all around. The smell of tear gas filled the air, yet this crowd remained eerily calm as they waited for someone to speak. Jackson assumed that the panthers were armed and scattered throughout the area but there was no voice of leadership to be heard. They had yet to determine exactly who the enemy might be. There was no Stokely Carmichael, no Bobby Seals, no Malcolm X, no Huey

Newton, no H. Rap Brown, Angela Davis, Jesse Jackson, Eldridge Cleaver and now . . . no Martin Luther King for peace. There was, however . . . an army of police cars that had began to arrive in the manner of the well trained riot police of Alabama. Fear began to fill the hearts of every black man and women in the crowd as the reality of violence edged closer and closer by the second. Just as it had during the marches down south in the early sixties, it seemed to creep along the ground and up into your soul. The kinks of hair on a black man's neck have a way of attempting to stand when eminent danger is upon them. The first natural impulse is to run but there is no place to run this time. In a matter of seconds you become a part of a mindless bunch of frightened people that have yet to realize that they are truly in danger.

The police had begun to assemble just a few blocks away. They were in clear view of the crowd that was now standing tightly together like a herd of cattle being prepared for slaughter. The police were armed and helmeted, they aligned shoulder to shoulder. Most of them stood tapping their nightsticks against their opposite hand in a well rehearsed ritual for what was about to occur. Others stood rigid like the plastic toy soldiers we all have played with as children. Their eyes were focused straight-ahead, legs wide apart and a cold uncaring gaze fixed upon their faces. They numbered approximately two hundred and growing. These young and overwhelmingly white policemen were about to face what was now a very frightened and uneasy crowd of blacks. Most of the blacks were here because they had stood all that they could humanly stand and had finally found the courage, or the folly, to challenge and resist the racist rules that had been crippling the hearts of a virtually submissive race of people. A choice had suddenly confronted all those who had balled and held their fist high above their head in defiance. Now was the time to fight or to find a place to hide.

Someone among the crowd began to shout, "They killed King! Now they want to beat us!" The young black man paced back and forth and began to gain confidence. No one knew him or where he was from. He made no Panther gestures or any other identifiable signs. "We're not going to run this time . . . we're not breaking any laws . . . they are the murderers, we're the people!" he shouted at the top of his lungs. There was still a relative silence as all eyes and ears were upon the young man now standing on the roof of a car raising his fist with hatred as he spoke. "King didn't do noth'n and they shot . . . him . . . down . . . We're tired of the abuse!" someone yelled, while raising his fist in the all too familiar Panther fashion, "Black Power to the people!" The crowd woke briefly and roared, "Black Power!" The man on the car roof continued to shout as loud as he could, "We want the police out of our neighborhoods . . . no more killing blacks . . . no more attack dogs . . . no more beatings in the streets!" The crowd began to mumble and yell sporadically, "Black Power! Whitey go home!"

The police were beginning to move in, this was it. This is where they were to stand up for their rights . . .

Overhead, the sudden roar of two military helicopters jolted most of the crowd to its knees. The down draft had enough pressure to knock an average man to the ground. With a whirlwind, hats, pieces of paper and dust were flying and swirling into the air. Most of the people, including the Panthers and the 409, crouched to the ground and began to quickly crawl towards any cover they could find. Within minutes tear gas canisters began to explode amidst them. The screams of women and perhaps of many men sent a final surge of fear into the panicking crowd. A wave of horse mounted Capital Policemen wearing gas mask began to prance their horses broadside and into the crowd. Just behind the wave of horse mounted police the lines of masked policemen on foot began to quickly move forward with shields and knight sticks in motion. The now scrambling and screaming crowd of men and women were on their feet and running away from the onslaught. Above the now constant sound of exploding tear canisters was the loud but muffled sound of a police bullhorn "Please disperse now! Move back out of the area! Leave this area immediately." The crowd of people began to stampede up Seventh Street. The feet of so many pounding in panic against the pavement sounded and felt as if the earth had chosen this particular moment to rumble and give way. The running crowd quickly grew larger and larger by the minute as they were forced northward away from downtown and into what was known as the ghettos. With the air still thick with dark smoke and tear gas, the tide began to change as shots rang out from within the human herd. Stones and bottles were rained down upon the pursuing policemen from every direction. The six militants and their comrades began to instinctively take a stance as the battle moved into the alleys and streets of the hood.

It didn't take long for the conflict to make its turn into chaos as the reckless and frightened crowd spontaneously changed its focus from survival to greed. All of the angry voices went silent as the sound of breaking storefront glass and metal gates were being kicked and pulled to the ground allowing access to a bounty of clothing and appliances. The three hour long battle found that the police had retreated to the safety of the downtown area while the soldiers of the streets became the looters and rioters of this elusive revolution. The young militants had lost . . . this was not a war and there would never be one. This was simply a blind reaction to a blind act of hatred.

The anguish and sadness of Martin Luther King's death had turned into the very thing that he had stood against. This final horizon was not one of a dream of equality; instead, it had turned into a nightmare of all the racial hatred that still lies ahead for a people who have yet to learn why. This was once again an emotionally demeaning defeat of a not so proud people; a people whose time had come and vanished within hours. Before the tear gas had cleared from their eyes, their hopes had simply fallen back to the painful tears of fear and uncertainty. They are still lie-in-wait for the next motive to stand-up and pretend that equality is a dream that is shared by everyone. They were caught in a frenzy of greed and carelessness. As the members gathered they headed for the abandoned police vehicles. Momentarily they pretended to be winning the war by destroying their cars and watching their retreat, as the blacks shot their guns into the morning air.

The streets now belonged to the people. Police cars were burning and billows of black smoke filled the air. Jackson passed the word on to his members to stay close and not leave the Seventh Street area, protect the people, and not to fire at anyone. The crowd and obviously some of the store owners began setting their places of business ablaze. Jackson, for one, realized that the perception of doom was wrong. We had been deceived. This is no Armageddon, this was not about racism; this was the true American way of getting what you could get. They had quickly forgotten the reason they were there. As the 409 walked through the crowds of looters in groups of ten they came across a crowd that had encircled two white policemen in the door way of clothing store. Their car had been over turned they appeared to have been beaten. Their clothes were torn and hanging, their weapons were missing, they were obviously afraid and little did they know there was no help coming. The crowd seemed to be talking to the two officers as Jackson and his comrades arrived into the center of the commotion. "You folks don't want to do this," one of the officers said, "we're policemen you could all be in serious trouble." At this point Jackson wasn't sure if they were trying to save their asses or for some reason trying to protect the clothing store.

A black girl in the crowd expressed her interest in an expensive red dress that was hanging in the display window.

"You want that dress baby?" asked Curt, who was apart of Jackson's group of armed blacks.

"Yes," she answered. Curt backed off and kicked the plate glass window. The window shattered and he calmly climbed into the display and handed the garment out to the now buzzing, but still unmoving crowd. It seemed to be the only store that hadn't been opened to the public. The policeman looked directly at Jackson and said, "Look, my wife's in there with other employees, please don't hurt them, just let us go." The sound of glass exploding was rapidly moving down the huge store front as people began to move into the window showcases. The policemen were running out of time

"Get inside," Jackson said to the officer. El-Tez and Jackson quickly went into the store. Once inside the two policemen herded the employees into one area near the front door. Jackson led them through the exit and escorted them to the next block and into an abandoned car. They packed into the car and drove off amidst the threats of the crowd . . . Just what kind of warriors were we, Jackson thought this was becoming more and more unclear. They abuse us, we protect them. Jackson's group began to assist folks who had stumbled or had gotten trapped in the turmoil. Most of the blocks were now ablaze and still no fire trucks in sight, and they weren't coming.

There was no reason to stay in the Seventh Street area. There was no reason to confront the police in the downtown area. Most of them had gotten involved in the looting, and those who hadn't had concluded that now was not the time to fight and that probably the time would never come. They were wrong. Those who were from Jackson's inner circle regrouped and headed by car through N.E. Washington to Minnesota Ave. S.E. to Nichols Avenue where traffic was blocked by abandoned and burning cars. The district police station was surrounded by blacks screaming and demanded the release of prisoners that had been gathered since last nights turmoil started. Policemen were in full riot gear protecting the police station from the rioters and began to respond. Tear gas was again fired into the crowds. The crowd began picking up and hurling the canister back at the police. The crowd and the police clashed at about twenty people deep just in front of Jackson and his men. With night sticks in hands and shields across their chest, the notorious policemen from this precinct were attacking unmercifully. Almost instantly Jackson was cut by a piece of flying glass, as a tear gas canister exploded in a store front window projecting pieces of glass into the crowd and into his left ankle. He was bleeding badly as the crowd began to stampede back away from the oncoming police. Jackson's comrades, with guns drawn, began to back off with him limping and in the center of the group. Without provocation Jimmy dragged a white man from his traffic jammed car and struck him with the butt of his shot gun. He then got into the car and drove up onto the sidewalk. Throwing Jackson inside, they changed drivers and drove onto Naylor Road and away from the war zone. Down the avenue towards Anacostia, Jackson could see the National Guards marching across the bridge on their way to trapping his people and the rioters between the police and guardsmen. With Jimmy in charge, Jackson knew there would be serious trouble if his boys were trapped. He knew they would surely shoot it out with the police. "Go back," he demanded, "We've got to get back to the guys." The driver made a U-turn and headed back down Naylor Road. As they came closer to what is now called Martin Luther King Boulevard, they heard a lot of gun fire. The National Guards had just cleared the bridge and were now running into the crowd. People were running towards their cars trying to escape up Naylor Road. Jackson got out of the car and stood bleeding on the sidewalk as the crowds pushed pass him screaming from the burning sensation of the tear gas. He could not see what was going on further up Nichols Ave. Part of a huge furniture store at the corner of Naylor Road and Nicholas Ave. was ablaze in addition to several small stores across the street. His guys were no where in sight. Jimmy suddenly came around the corner and into Jackson's view. He was running up the opposite side of the street and firing back at the national guards. The panic crowd instinctively fell to the ground as the gun shots filled the air. The others were still out of sight or perhaps had gone another way. As Jackson yelled and gestured to Jimmy, who was running in another direction, to hurry, his chest suddenly exploded. He was first lifted off of the ground by the impact of the bullet and then dropped and tumbled over the backs of those that were crouched down against the concrete sidewalk. Within seconds the guardsmen had caught up to him and were now standing over him with weapons pointed down at his face. As Jackson ran towards his fallen comrade his sense of fear escaped him just as it had so many times throughout his life. Amidst the panicked and screaming crowd, the armed national guardsmen pointed their weapons directly at Jackson demanding that he stop and keep away. Jimmy had been blown out of both his shoes, which were lying where he had gotten hit by gun fire. One of his legs from the knee down was facing upwards as he laid face down on the sidewalk. Without obvious reasons the guardsmen began to back up away from Jackson as he continued to approach. The guardsmen began to refocus their attention to the confusion back around the corner where the police had corralled most of the rioters. There were men and women lying face down with their hands strapped behind their backs while police and national guardsmen stood with guns pointed at them as prisoners. The voices were booming "get back or you will be arrested or shot". During the commotion Jackson made his way to his fallen comrade. Jimmy was lying face down in a pool of his own blood. With the words 'oh no' upon his lips, Jackson bent over and tried to lift Jimmy's limp body from the side walk. Shockingly, as he reached and put his hands under Jimmy, his right hand slipped into the bloody hollow cavity of Jimmy's chest. Startled, he quickly yanked his hand back out. "Oh my God" he whispered. He found that jimmy's insides had been blown completely out by the gun shot. They had lost one of their own in a way he had never dreamed. The others were still no where in sight . . .

Later he arrived at the apartment of a female friend just before dark. Using her phone, Jackson called all the phone numbers of the key inner circle members trying to locate Fred. Everyone who hadn't been arrested was to meet at Barnaby Terrace to regroup if something went wrong. The female friend helped bandage Jackson's wound and volunteered to drive them back to Barnaby Terrace before the eight o'clock curfew, which had been broadcast on all the local radio and television channels

As they drove away and reached the Goodhope Road section of S.E. Washington, they saw that the national guards had secured Sears Roebuck and the shopping mall located across the street. There were no people, fires or any type of disturbance, unlike a half mile down the street. Down there behind them all hell had broken loose. The smoke and tear gas that made its way up the hill was the only indication that all wasn't well in the Nations capital. This intersection was a divide line between an all black area and a divided white community. As they quickly drove toward Wheeler Road, they witnessed scattered groups of blacks roaming near major intersections and smoldering shopping plazas. They turned onto Wheeler Road which leads to Barnaby Terrace. Wheeler Road liquor store was partially gutted along with the remaining block of small businesses such as a dry cleaners, a corner store and laundry mat, yet across the street a recently built bank and hardware store was untouched. Once they topped Wheeler Road towards the Maryland state line, they could go no further. The Maryland state police and national guards had again secured another area that separated those that have and those that don't. It seemed that their idea of containing the area was to let the blacks tear up all that they did not want, as long as it was inside the poverty stricken areas. Jackson and his group along with many other so called black movement groups had been used. The long term plan to publicly 'stand up and fight the man' or 'stand up and fight for rights', had been terminated by the assassination that by design, would result in an unplanned futile riots and burnings with-in their own community and only their own community. Jackson and his group's organized posturing and threats of doing something real were falling apart. Their plan of following the organized movement had exploded the moment the fatal shot was fired. Now they had no plan . . . now they were recklessly reacting to the 'last straw'. Instead of defending themselves against abuse and mistreatment with the help of fair-minded whites, they were caught up in the widening of the gap between those that they needed who were sympathetic to the struggle

Jackson's feelings that the world was ending on this day were diminishing quickly. He began to realize that there will be many tomorrows and each would get worse as time marched on. They no longer had a cause. They, the white race, had again proven that blacks were no threat. They can assassinate our leader, we'll respond by shooting ourselves in the foot. From N.W. Washington through N.E. and all the way to the far end of S.E. was the same scene. They just simply tore up their own cage. Business will be the same . . . if not better, for those who pissed into the cage and onto the people that harmlessly stomp and cry.

"Only God can help us; maybe religious people are right."

Once they were back at Barnaby Terrace Jackson felt safe, this was home, this was where his comrades could regroup, lick their wounds and start all over. On April 4, 1968 Jackson was 22 years old, now April 5, twenty four hours later, he felt at lease twenty years older and aging. How stupid could they have been to think they could get the attention of the giant and not be stomped upon. We are not a warring people. We are a people of compassion, we can not win

They were greeted by about thirty friendly faces, each telling their own stories and asking what had happened to others. As Jackson mingled through the crowd he noticed that some of the men and women he loved and trusted were missing. There was no Eddie Brooks, no El-Tez, no Curt, and no Fred

"Has anybody seen Eddie Brooks?" Jackson asked. Someone came forward and told what had happened on Nichols Avenue after he had left. As he began to speak, most of the others gathered closely to listen. "While we were gathered on the fringes of the crowd, the police began firing tear gas into the center of it. The crowd began running back down Nichols Ave. Most of us began walking along the store fronts, still armed and pretty much caught in the middle of all the confusion. There was a long line of cars stuck in traffic, most of them were empty, but some stupid whiteys decided to stay with their cars. Jimmy Warren dragged a man out of his car. The man objected until Jimmy butted him with his shot gun.

"As you know", he said nodding and looking at Jackson, "Once Jimmy commandeered the car he turned it around and drove it right onto the sidewalk where you and Eddie Richardson got in and drove off. Then someone spotted the national guardsmen coming up Nichols Ave., trapping everybody in between the police coming down the street and the national guards coming up. The police were constantly firing tear gas. All of a sudden Jimmy began firing his shot gun like crazy. Eddie Brooks, El-Tez and me kicked in the front door of that fruit store and went inside to clear our heads. Jimmy, Curt and Smitty were in the middle of the street in front of us. Jimmy busted another white man's car window opened the door and told the man to get out. The driver wouldn't get out but the two passengers got out of the back of the car and ran down the street towards the on-coming guards. The driver was still resisting and holding on to his steering wheel while Jimmy and now Smitty, were attempting to drag the man out. Curt had punched the other passenger and removed him from the front seat and got into the car. The man Curt had pulled out of the front passenger seat had grabbed a piece of pipe or something and was attempting to smash the passenger side window where Curt was sitting. After his first swing, Jimmy, from the other side of the car, fired his shotgun hitting the man in the chest. People were screaming and running in all directions. Jimmy fired again, this time at the legs of the driver, that had started to run. He was going crazy. People, seeing the blood and the shotgun still blasting, now into the air, began falling to the ground and covering their heads. Jimmy got into the car and was trying to drive up onto the sidewalk to get out of there, when the police approached and began shooting into the car. Curt got out of the car and we called him into the store with us. I don't know where Smitty went but Jimmy had ducked behind the car and was reloading his shotgun. The police had walked up on Jimmy and told him to get down on the ground. They told everybody to get down on the ground or be shot. Jimmy stood up and fired and ran down the sidewalk. The police were giving chase and firing as they went by us. We kicked the rear door of the store open and escaped out into the alley and walked back here. It all happened in a few short seconds, I mean there was nothing we could do", he said.

"Where's Eddie and El-Tez?" Jackson asked.

"They're in your apartment; Jean wanted to know where you were, we told her that you had got away, but we didn't know where you had gone and that you were bleeding", he answered.

Jackson was breathing easier knowing Eddie and El-Tez made it back. As he walked away from the small crowd and down the sidewalk onto the steps leading to his apartment, he stopped and took a moment to digest toady's events. Just inside the door was Gloria, now six months pregnant with his third daughter and an apartment full of comrades that meant the world to him; all unsure of what might happen next and all in danger of being swallowed up by the misfortunes that come with the changing of a nation

He thought briefly of Jimmy Warren, who was the first of his inner circle to loose his life and the life of perhaps the innocent man he had taken. He wondered if he hadn't gotten cut, would he have died beside Jimmy? He wondered if he had been protected by some sort of guardian angel, in light of the number of times he had been shot at and now these two deaths that occurred could have easily been him instead of them. Even more importantly, he thought about what their next step would be. What measures do we need to take to survive what might be coming next. He was more of a worried child than a ferocious warrior. He entered into his friend filled apartment to the outstretched arms of his sweetheart and the high five hand slapping that indicates the happy greeting of a comrade. After a short assuring conversation with Jean a group of them returned to the parking area to discuss what's next. The sirens were still sounding in the distant. The night was still lit by the glow of structural fires burning up on Wheeler Road. As mentioned early, the Maryland state and Prince George's county police were in abundance just on the other side of our building and not more than three hundred yards away

For them there was no interest in looting, they were more in agreement to focus on attempting to move the police and guards off of their doorstep without loss of another life, while they were still under the cover of darkness

Two men, with rifles and walkie-talkies in hand, were placed on the roof of Barnaby Terrace where they had a good view of the area and an easy escape route to the ground. Two others were place on both ends of the complex facing the Maryland State line. If gunfire occurred, they were positioned to return fire at the vehicles, but instructed not to fire on humans. They began to move as a growing group and then a crowd, out onto Wheeler Road S.E. and to start marching toward South Capital Street to the awaiting line of police cars. Within a few moments the crowds had grown just as they had earlier, to thousands, most were coming from local ten block area of ghettos. Looters were still doing their unruly breaking of windows and disrupting what little traffic there was. At their backs they had pushed several old cars into the middle of Wheeler Road and set them on fire to prevent being trapped again. It was now about 11:00pm, the huge crowd was still growing in size and was now at the corner of Wheeler Road and Southern Avenue where it had come face to face with the Maryland police who were crouched behind rows of parked cars, buses and trucks. Fire trucks were being positioned to turn the hoses onto the crowd if they became unruly. A police bull horn screeched and then sounded into the night air. "You people are in violation of the curfew, this area has been declared into 'a state of emergency', you have ten minutes to clear the area or you will be arrested or shot. Go home now!" Again, he repeated the message. Before the message could be repeated a third time a few people began to throw rocks at the police. The crowd followed suit, hurling stones, bricks, and anything else that could be used against the police. Cocktails were thrown into cars parked in the area in attempt to get the firemen to direct their hoses to the fires instead of the people. As expected the tear gas came first, bursting and exploding along the ground and into our crowd. Then came the water hoses of only two stationed fires trucks, neither was enough. The crowd scrambled and surged into the policed area as it attempted to escape the clouds of tear gas. Clashes of police and blacks were occurring all through the ranks with the police being badly out numbered and the crowd being protected by the night.

The exchange of gas canisters and rocks went on for at least ten long minutes. And then; suddenly the two forces began to separate without reason. The police began pulling off as the crowd began to retreat back into the District of Columbia, still rampaging as it moved again back down Wheeler Road. As the police and guardsmen moved out, gun fire erupted into the air and shots rang out from the surrounding buildings and from the crowd. Jackson's own roof top gunners did not fire a shot and reported that the police and guardsmen had retreated into a shopping area just off the Maryland side of Wheeler Road. The crowd, seemingly happy with their position inside the district line shifted their attention back to looting. Most of Jackson men, that didn't get caught up into the looting, including himself, retreated back to Barnaby Terrace.

All night the sirens cried out indicating an ongoing turmoil. The continuing smell of tear gas and burning wood still filled the air throughout the night of April 5, 1968.

On the morning of April the 6th, the overview of Wheeler Road was that of a city that appeared to have been hit by a bomb. Most of the storefront buildings were still smoldering. Some areas, where buildings once stood, were now just piles of brick between standing partition walls. In the district, there were no policemen in sight. Across the Maryland state-line the congregation of National Guard and policemen were again beginning to grow as far as the eye could see into Maryland. There were all types of police and military armed and armored vehicles just idling, poised and prepared to stop any further uprising. The chance of generating another raging crowd was gone. As white folks used to say about us and roaches, most of the people "disappeared into the woodwork." What had occurred last night seemed to be a part of a dream or nightmare with these exceptions, lives were permanently changed and landscapes were gone forever.

They had no way to communicate with members who didn't live inside their area. Phone service was disrupted or disconnected. Most electric power had been shut down and there was no food source. One nearby market had been burned down and the other was now used as the headquarters for the national guards. Needless to say those who did not loot for edible foods, including Jackson, or have food stored, were going to suffer some hungry times. At Barnaby Terrace they all laid low and rested waiting for another night to fall and give them the cover needed to go out and find food.

After a day of planning the next steps they divided into groups of five and headed out into the neighborhood to scavenge for food and drink and to find out what if anything was being done in the nearby complexes. For the next three days they ate and drank from foods that were brought back off of the nightly runs into the streets and burnt out stores. They were lucky enough to savage about ten cases of mackerel that had survived a burnt and over turned food delivery truck. One of the nightly runs brought back the news that, one panther strong hold had been raided by F.B.I. agents and more then fifty members had been arrested. More importantly it was said that they had federal warrants for a long list of wanted men including, Jackson Thomas, Edward Brooks, Ronald Allen (El-Tez), Curtis Toler and others. The warrants supposedly were issued for crimes ranging from murder, inciting to riot, or transporting illegal weapons across state lines.

On April 9, 1968 they were awaken at 4:00 a.m. by one of the look-out men that had been stationed on the roof. He warned that, the national guard had moved up and in front of Barnaby Terrace and eight or nine unmarked cars were now parked on one side and in front of Barnaby in addition to about thirty armed state police in riot gear standing at the southern entrance. Jackson immediately began to evacuate his people from the building by using the planned exit route that led past the rear parking lot where the D.C. police had just began to assemble a group of patty wagons and policemen, also in riot gear. Most of Jackson's group had safely gotten into a nearby apartment building where they could see from the rear view windows. The police and agents were raiding the Barnaby Complex. With flood lights pointing onto every exit they ordered everyone out of the building and to come out one at a time with hands held above their heads. After being laid down and searched they were questioned and released or loaded onto the waiting patty wagons. Jackson saw his apartment patio window busted down and entered with guns drawn as they rushed in to what was now just an empty apartment loaded with weapons and other goods including all of his furniture and clothing.

All that day they laid-low and spent most of their time saying good byes to one another. They knew they could not possibly hide such a large group of men and women even in the heart of the ghettos. They began their exits one or two at a time. Eddie Brooks and another member, left and headed for Newark, New Jersey, where he had relatives. El-Tez and Paula were put on a bus to Philadelphia. Curt and Eddie Richardson headed for Columbus Ohio. Jackson and Jean left Washington and went to Cleveland. Others went to different cities with a plan to regroup after the heat was off. Freddie Morris stayed in the Washington area along with some members that didn't have arrest warrants issued for them.

On April 12, 1968 Jackson and Jean arrived safely in Cleveland and had made refuge at his sister's home. The following days were unhappy and laden with worry as to what may have happened to all of the men and women that they had spent so much time with, and wondering if some were dead or alive. They had all agreed that they would not attempt to contact each other while in hiding. Now they were divided and on their own. Not quite knowing what had gone wrong so quickly or exactly how they would ever be able to totally regroup.

On April the 30th Jackson was sitting in his sister's living room with Jean, and his three nieces when a friend of his sister's knocked on the rear door and informed him that there were two unmarked police cars parked at the end of the street and that they had been asking questions about who occupied this house. Not wanting to frighten Jean or his sister's children, Jackson put his shoes on and walked down to the corner. There were, as the man said, two unmarked cars with Ohio tags, with two white men in each car. They appeared to be policemen, except the cars were more dilapidated than a typical police car and they appeared to be drinking from bottles of alcohol and at one point one of them got out of the car and threw up his food, pissed and got back into the car. After an hour of watching from the bushes Jackson walked out onto the sidewalk and up to one of the cars.

"Do you know what time it is?" he asked through an open passenger side window. Someone inside the car answered,

"Yeah Jackson, and you niggers aint got much time left." This stranger who Jackson had never seen called him by his first name. He did not react or make any comment to the men, being so outnumbered. As he slowly walked away keeping an eye on both cars as he got out of view, he didn't know what to make of this encounter. He didn't know who they were or who they represented, how they knew his first name or what they could possibly want. He went back into the house and continued to peek out the window. At around 9:00pm the cars started and they drove away, still puzzled by the incident Jackson was able to breath a lot easier after the cars were gone.

They had been sitting in the living room for about an hour after the cars had left when the front windows seemed to explode inwardly followed by a crashing sound at the front door. He grabbed the children and fell to the floor while the windows continued to be knocked out. After a few quiet moments of fear, a knock came from the back door. He reluctantly crawled toward the back door looking for something to protect himself on the way. The red reflection of a police flashing light was hitting on and off on the unlit walls of the living room. The knock came again this time even harder, a voice spoke through the door, "open up its the police." The children were crying aloud and Jean was now moaning loudly as if she had been hit and injured.

"Who are you and what do you want," Jackson asked.

"We're the police, are you folks all right?" came another voice from the front through the shattered window. Flash lights were now shinning into the house as more police cars began to arrive. Once inside they looked around and began to make sarcastic remarks about the incident. One of the policemen asked if Jackson knew why anyone would want to harm him or his family. Jackson answered, "I have no idea who or why anyone in Cleveland might want to harm us." another officer remarked that, "Whoever it was, was frightened off when our police cars just happened to drive onto the street and spot the two cars driving onto your front lawn. I would speculate that it was a random racist act following the riots that have burned parts of Cleveland. They must have did this because you live here in our white community. You might want to move yourselves back into your own ghetto before someone gets hurt," he said with a wink and a slight grin on his face.

Gloria was now obviously in pain and asking for help as Jackson had no choice but to turn on the lights to see what damage had been done and to make sure Gloria and the others had not been hurt. He was holding her tightly in his arms and trying to gather and hold the children at the same time.

"Call an ambulance; something is wrong with my girlfriend!" The police responded and with-in minutes the ambulance arrived and took Jean to the hospital with Jackson at her side. At the hospital emergency room they determined that Jean had gone into labor, the next morning Jackson's third daughter was born three months premature but both the baby and Jean were okay considering what they had both gone through.

After two months in Cleveland and a constant flow of racial acts to live with, Jackson made contact with Fred Morris in Washington. With him saying that things had cooled down and the inner circle was beginning to come back together, Jackson and Jean gathered their newborn daughter named Sandy and headed back to Washington D.C. It was mid June 1968, they temporarily moved in with Fred into Stanton Gardens S.E. Washington, the one strong hold area of black that escaped untouched by the riots. Fred and Jimmy Gylipsy lived in the same apartment building and both men understood the movement and why there was still hope of making change by hook or crook.

After the riots the politicians in Washington decided the old way of racism wasn't working. The effort was under way to rebuild Washington. There were still warrants for the arrest of Jackson and many of his comrades.

A new type of racism wasted no time finding its way to the planning tables of the invisible, but mighty machine. They wanted changes in the laws. They wanted more prisons and they wanted them filled with blacks. This was an answer to eliminate not only deserving criminals but also blacks that believe that change can only be achieved by force. Beating blacks on the streets wasn't working because there were too many whites that believed that the John Lynch idea of abusive intimidation was not a Christian thing to do. They began to realize that the black race, just like their own race, has its share of good and bad people and that if whites continued to blatantly treat them like dirt, sooner or later they were going to learn to kill as a part of their own racial hatred.

Chapter 20

Within thirty days of being back in D.C., Jackson had acquired a new identification, a social security number, a drivers license and a new job working for Chesapeake Potomac Electric Company as a specialist for repairing oil circuit breakers. He and his family were back on track and quickly falling into a normal life with hopes that maybe the death of Martin Luther King had caused a changed. Black policemen were being hired. Those already on the force had begun to be moved up in rank. The black officers had even begun to ride in squad cars along with their white counterparts. That alone was a major step in a different direction. Racist police were being charged with abuse and no longer free to use the street Gestapo tactics they had used prior to the riots. They began to give a little respect to blacks because of the threat that we may be more courageous than they had thought. Maybe, just as they spat on us we would begin to spit back. The likes of Martin Luther King performed in a way that was acceptable to the white society. That being that, their notion of the right way for blacks to respond to racism is to retaliate with peaceful protest and humble biblical remedies for any violent racial infractions against our people. For a moment during the riots it felt and looked as if brutality and discrimination would no longer be tolerated by blacks under thirty. For a brief moment it looked as if we may open our eyes and build our courage enough to respond to violence just as they do. And they have done it with so much success. They rule the world with violence and weaponry while we respond to abuse with the kiss of forgiveness and a dream of all men becoming equal . . . someday. They applaud our submissiveness while lashing out with all of the subliminal hatred they can bestow and in a kind way, of course, calling us stupid and unappreciative fools. None of our circle of freedom seekers respected the ways of white men or anyone else that suggested that we remain as we are and learn to hope and to be thankful for what we will receive in the next kingdom for our willingness to sacrifice our blood, swet and tears in return for the blessing of humbleness and a place with God. It seemed to Jackson that racism itself took on a new disguise in 1968. Racists were willing to give us the satisfaction of knowing that we sent them a message and they heard it loud and clear. They made Martin Luther King a Christ like martyr while the segregation and discrimination he preached against remained the same and in many ways worst . . . Now we have pacification along with our segregated and discriminative life styles. They assured us easier access to drugs rather than jobs. They re-instituted to an ultimate level of what it means to be educated, as if a lack of schooling was the reason for the economic differences between the races. They pronounced that the dreams of the poor were about to come true and all men will be judged by the content of his character and not the color of his skin . . . and yet there they were with an income level of nearly half that of the average white uneducated male.

Jackson received a long distant call out of Chicago. The incoming voice came from a well known leader of an underground group of activist known as J.D.L. The call went something like this.

"We understand you guys are doing some good things for your cause. We've got a good tip on some dollars that I know, the movement can use . . . you know . . . to feed the children, buy some winter clothes or some needed medical supplies, you interested?"

"Yes," was the answer on this side of the phone connection. "Listen; head north on 70 near Frederick there's a Dairy Company, as you will see the dairy trucks parked on the docks on the right hand side of the highway. The burglar alarm will be shut off this Friday night. The outer gate which I normally chained and padlocked will have a open padlock. Be sure to throw it away when you are done. Pull in the open slot between two dairy delivery trucks. The company safe will be on the dock and ready to go. We think it will be 15 to 20 thousand in cash inside from the weeks take. You guys owe us big time on this bro, we'll call you next week for an arms hit on 40 West so stay tuned, right on brothers, power to the people."

Jackson was reluctant about becoming involved again, even if it meant a lot to the cause. He wanted to enjoy the peace of mind that came with a descent job and a new apartment for his family. Even so, on Friday, four of them headed north very excited about the potential dollars sitting for the taking. They took two cars, one being a look-out car with a walkie-talkie in case something went wrong. With the lookout car in place three of them entered into the gate just after dark. With the car lights out they headed toward the rear docks. They could see the constant flow of traffic heading north and south out on the interstate that was just about 300 yards and on the other side of a ten foot wire fence. We cautiously backed between the two trucks as directed, shut off the motor, sat for a moment checking to make sure the look-out car could hear our call. The coast was clear, "Let's do it," was the command.

After opening the trunk we searched the dock and found the safe, exactly where they had said it would be.

"Damn, look at the size of this sucker," came from the voice of one of the team.

"I don't think its gon'na fit in the trunk." "It's got to, we don't have a choice," came a response. The safe was about three feet wide by five foot high. Our thought was that we could gently drop it into the trunk leaving the bottom stick out the back about two feet that we could cover and tie the trunk door down covering all but a small piece of the safe. As the three of them tilted the top of the safe toward the trunk the weight, which was about 1000 pounds, was too much to handle. The safe suddenly crashed into the trunk wedging the lid of the trunk up into a vertical position and wide open. Frantically they tried to pull the safe back enough to release the trunk lid, to no avail. "Pull the safe up quick," someone shouted. The car was moved forward with the rear bumper now nearly touching the ground. They tried desperately to pry the safe back out but it was solidly wedge and could not be moved. Now in a panic, Jackson got into the car and drove out of the gate up to the look out car where they again tried without success to move the safe. Suddenly three Maryland state police cars roared past them heading for and entering the gate that they had just exited just about a quarter of a mile down the road. As they pulled into position around the dairy company another police car roared by without noticing the two cars, one behind another with the four of them ducked down out of site.

Since it was his car Jackson drove off the side street with the three others right behind him in the other car. Onto the interstate he drove with the bottom of the car occasionally scraping the ground with sparks and a loud grinding noise every time he hit a slight dip. With his comrades still in the side view mirror they sped along at about ninety miles per hour trying to get away as other police cars with their lights flashing were across the highway headed in the opposite direction. In his rear view mirror all he could see was the top of the trunk lid. The blanket covering the bottom half of the safe had blown off leaving nearly half the safe in plain view and still with the lid wedged straight up and wide open. He took the first available exit, knowing they would not make the long trek back to Washington D.C. Once off the highway they drove along a dark country road looking for a turn off where they could regroup and decide the next step. Finally, he turned onto a grassy side road leading through a cow pasture and down onto a dead-end path with his comrades still faithfully trailing behind. They turned the car lights off hoping no one had spotted them. They knew they had to get the safe out of the car before daybreak or they would be doomed. With a log that they found lying nearby they pried for nearly an hour before the safe finally came loose. Knowing that they couldn't leave it in the middle of the path Jackson got back into the car and backed down what appeared in the moonlight to be a bushy area at the end of the trail. Under cover of the darkness of night they gave the safe one final pry. It came out of the trunk and into a small clump of bushes. As the safe hit the ground it landed unevenly and tumbled over once and it rocked a little and quickly tumbled down what turned out to be an embankment. It rolled downward picking up speed as it went. They stood helplessly in the night as the safe crashed through the brush and came to rest by splashing into a creek at the bottom of the hill. The creek was about five feet deep and it seemed to enjoy swallowing their newly taken fortune. Dumbfounded and yet momentarily relieved, they all sat laughing in the dark wondering how their luck could be so bad.

The next day they all pitched in and rented a u-haul truck. They bought ropes and pulleys and picked up two additional men and headed back to their treasure very well prepared. The local radio news made mention of the burglary of the dairy which netted the thieves well over twenty thousand dollars. They continued on their journey with three men in the front and four in the back. They sang along the way as if going on a camping expedition. Using the pulley and a lot of brute strength they managed to get the safe up and out of the water and into the truck while a small herd of cattle looked on as if they knew that we were up to no good. They seemed to be minding their own business, quietly watching and chewing the whole three or four hours that it took. During the drive back to Washington they were again singing and full of joy knowing that they were loaded with the white man's cash. They made jokes of the caper and done the typical hand slapping knowing they were the bosses of crime.

Once they arrive back at the apartment complex they hooked up an extension cord, plugged in a power drill and went to work. Drilling and pounding on the rear wall of the safe that was now lying on its side.

Throughout the night they worked until getting tired and heading inside for a little rest. Early the next morning, after a night of deciding how they would divvy the bounty to so many people, Jackson went out alone and climbed back into the truck, sat down in front of the door side of the safe and turned the handle for the first time only to find that it was never locked. The safe was still lying on it's side and as soon as he turned the handle the heavy door slammed open against the floor exposing all the little shelves and drawers and a big empty space at the bottom. It was empty! There was nothing, no papers, no money, no checks, nothing but dust. It was as if it had been empty for years. When he went back into the apartment to inform the guys, they rushed out in disbelief.

"No way after all the risk and all the money we spent for a truck and tools, how could this safe be empty?" Some of them thought that Jackson had taken the money for himself but none the less, like most dreams of riches, you always awake to find your hands and pockets just as empty as they were when you fell off to sleep.

Maybe someday we'll all realize that being able to dream is as rich as one can possibly get . . . then again, I say . . . to be rich without the ability to dream leaves a man's heart empty, so, enjoy the dream . . .

When the poor commit crimes against the poor they stand accused and often are sent to prison. When the poor commit crimes against the rich they are deemed to be ungodly and disgusting. When the rich rob the masses by deception and manipulation they are most often within the law. When they can no longer benefit by that law they take credit for changing that law. When the masses cry out for justice in exchange for peace, the rich cry out for fairness in exchange for charity.

Chapter 21

Was the lead from our dairy delight that turned into a dairy disaster, a set-up?

Did they take the wrong safe off the dock, as it was later explained? If so, what happened to the money?

The next Chicago call came less than a month after the first.

"What did you guys do with all that dairy loot," was the opening question. After Jackson informed them of the dollar-less fiasco they acted shocked and surprised that something could have gone wrong and suggested that we must have taken the wrong safe off the dock or something of that nature.

"If you guys can't handle a gift, what are we gon'na do with you." His remark was borderline offensive and not taken as funny, none the less," he said, we've got another one for you that's even better.

"There's a liquor supply store on Route 40 West just near Frostburg MD."

"No liquor man, we don't need liquor!"

"No, listen to me," he paused as if to adjust is statement.

"What I need to tell you is that there is cash and weapons that the clan intends on using against blacks and Jews. You know what I mean? We're going to cut the electrical power to the area on Sunday night, try and get there around midnight. There's a small window on the side of the building about six feet off the ground all the rest of the entries and exits are locked down with metal bars and might still be alarmed by battery." With the information given to Jackson he called a closed inner circle meeting to determine if this was real or maybe a worst set-up. A few of the 409 drove to the building the following day which was a Thursday.

The structure was a huge liquor store and warehouse that was open for business with what appeared to be a fireworks plant attached to the rear section. There were no other buildings for at least a mile in either direction. One power line was strung for about a hundred yards as the source of electricity. There doors had welded iron gates on a sliding track as a locking device. All the windows but the one on the right had one inch bars. The one small window was about twelve inches wide and about two feet high. It appeared to have had bars, but for some reason they had been cut and about a two inch nipple remained where the bars met the metal frame. The window was about six feet off the ground just as our Chicago voice had said, with this information we made the approximate two and a half hour trip back to D.C. We were skeptical about the whole situation, but with a call to Chicago it was confirmed that the source was from the weathermen and that one of the business owners was an inside informant. It was noted that the rear of this structure was a wooded downward sloped hillside without a roadway. The only way to approach the building was using Route 40. With two lookout vehicles a mile in either direction we would be safe for at least a few minutes if anything went wrong. They were still skeptical especially since they had yet to figure out just how the police were alerted at the dairy company which had resulted in their nearly being trapped inside the gates.

The stage was set, they decided just for safety they would not wait until midnight, they would strike at 9:30 pm just after dark. The line-up was two cars with walkie-talkies as lookouts, a U-haul truck, that was scheduled to arrive at 9:30pm, giving us time to remove the goods and place them behind the building to be loaded. One lookout in front of the building with a walkie-talkie and six men inside. The inside men were Freddie Morris, his younger brother Ritchie, Eddie Brooks, El-Tez, a new man and Jackson. They drove to Pittsburgh that morning taking one more look as they passed the building and headed homeward. Once in Pittsburgh they met up with Brooks and El-Tez. They rented the U-haul in a fictitious name for a one-way trip to D.C. Jackson picked up an old car his mother had given him that she was getting ready to junk and they were off and heading for their targeted destination. They left Pittsburgh in a three vehicle caravan, to D.C., with one stop in mind. The truck with one driver was parked about two miles from the destination where the driver was to wait for the proper time and the remaining seven of us continued on. After dropping the five of us at the target we waited until the look- outs drove away in both directions as far as they could go without losing radio contact. Once they were in place we headed one by one through the side window. Once inside we briefly gathered and headed off in different directions looking first for the money room, as it had been described as an area where they stored weapons. As Jackson prowled around looking for the money room he walked into a thin thread-like string that had been, for some reason strung across a walkway about one hundred feet from the window we had entered through. Not thinking very much of it, he continued on with his flashlight in hand, while constantly talking to the team, letting everyone know they were here together. Just before reaching the office area and the assumed money room Jackson felt another thin thread like string break against his leg about knee high, he knew instantly that something was wrong. Panicking, he ordered, "everybody out'ta here something's wrong!" he was yelling at the top of my lungs. "Let's go, go, go, come on, get out." Everyone was scrambling, climbing up the wall out the small window. Once outside we grabbed the lookout and walked across the highway where they gathered, panting and coughing from the frantic exit. They called both lookouts. They acknowledged that everything was clear.

"What's up," Jackson was asked by Fred. Why are you spooked?"

"I walked through two thread lines crossing the walkways as I went toward the money room and my past foolishness taught me that those might have been alarm lines, once broken they would let someone know we're here."

"What ta-f—," the unnamed new man said, "we did all that running cause you felt a piece of thread? That's bullshit."

"Well let's wait for awhile to see if anyone shows up." Jackson said. Fred and everyone else began to get restless, as the call kept coming back, "The coast is clear, no rollers."

They went back across the highway and paused at the window entry.

"I don't like this Fred," Jackson said."

"What do you want to do?" he asked. Someone answered for Jackson, "Let's just do it! Let Jackson be the lookout if he's scared." Jackson was not accustom to those kinds of accusations coming from his own homeboys. But this was a new member Jackson didn't even know his name. For a moment Brooks and a couple of the others stared at the fool and seemed to be about to jump in and set him straight but Jackson spoke up and said, "Alright, what do you guys want to do?" Someone other than the idiot said "lets do it, we've come to far to turn back, unless your sure the lines were burglar alarms and they don' seem to have been, since there's no pigs here by now."

"Okay, but the moment we get a signal that something is wrong I want everybody out immediately and without hesitation." With that, Fred entered the window followed by his brother Ritchie and the others. Jackson stayed outside as a lookout, not due to fear as the man accused but because he had a hunch that he could play a stronger part standing guard. While waiting not more 15 minutes Jackson began to get fidgety, he needed to be inside with his comrades. It was a clear cool night and the sky was bright and lit up the area nearly enough to see a couple hundred yards away. Jackson walked out to the highway and glanced in both directions. It was so quite that he could hear the car tires hitting the seams in the road long after they had gone out of sight. He used the walkie-talkie to check and make sure everything was still all clear, it was confirmed. Being outside was not for him even if he was uneasy. He decided to go back in. As he walked toward the side of the building where the entry window was located he noticed what seemed to be the light from a cigarette. Of course that would be nearly impossible; that someone would be down in the ravine in the middle of the forest smoking a cigarette. Jackson stood still and kept his eyes on the spot that he had seen the light. Again, something glowed and dimmed. This time he watched as the light moved upward and glowed brightly and then appeared to be swung down towards some ones waist as the glow diminished. We're being watched he said to himself. Then again he thought that it may be a firefly but he couldn't be sure. He continued to focus his sight on the area only to see another and then another. They couldn't be fireflies, they weren't flashing they were more like quickly cooled ambers. It was time to panic. They had been set up. Jackson back up to the window and yelled inside for everyone to come out. At he same time he called on the walkie-talkie for the car and truck to get on the move and pick them up. It was to late; within seconds the wooded area lit up with the single headlights of off road motor bikes He counted four and then five, six, seven, eight, this was a trap. Jackson began screaming into the window. "Get out! Get out now! It's a trap! We've been set up!" Suddenly the motors were roaring all over the valley below and getting closer and closer by the second. Jackson continued to scream out with urgency for his men to get out of the building. Boom, boom, came the sound of exploding shot guns from the rear side of the building. The sounds of the motor bikes and the blasting shotguns were coming up out of the wooded hillside down behind the building. Boom, boom, boom, shot after shot was being fired. The glass windows behind the bars were being shattered by the shot gun pellets. The sound of the motors were now seemingly coming from all over. The cycle lights could now be seen as they began to exit the brush onto the gravel surface. We were unarmed, but they could not have distinguished all the shooting as their own, yet they came like gang busters, without fear, spinning the gravel and shooting out their own windows.

"Get out, come out of there!" Jackson was still shouting. The first three had gotten out and ran across the roadway. "Come on man, come on. Ritchie's upper body had just come through the opening, Come on! Come on! Come on!" Jackson repeated as he pulled at Ritchie as hard as he could while wanting to run to safety himself. Ritchie had gotten seriously stuck on one of the upward bar nipples

"Come on." Jackson was now pleading as more cycles were coming up onto the gravel. Fred suddenly burst through the opening pushing Ritchie out and in front of him. They briefly hit the ground and were back up in a flash. The three of them was headed into the wooded area just to the right of where the cyclist had come from.

The shotguns were still exploding, but now all they could hit was each other. From the wooded area Jackson got on the walkie-talkie and told the car heading north towards Pittsburgh to "pick up our guys and don't stop until you get to my mother's house. He called to the truck to immediately get out of the area. The last call was for them to be picked up about a mile east of the target, in the clunker his mother had given him with the Pennsylvania licenses plate. As they made it to the highway, a car was coming along slowly flashing its lights to let us know to step out in view. They jumped in knowing that this wasn't over. The driver told them that there must have been twenty or so motor cycles surrounding the building, with their lights lighting up the whole front as he drove by, "What the fuck happened? Where did they come from?"

Jackson jumped into the driver's seat and headed east toward D.C. as fast as the old car could go. The police cars heading the opposite way were now passing them as they drove east. After four or five miles on the highway, they passed a parked state police vehicle that was sitting with just the parking lights on. After a few seconds and just as he was rounding a turn and getting out of view. He could see through the rear view mirror that the headlights of the police car had popped on. He was definitely in pursuit of them.

As they rounded a bend out of sight of the pursuing police car Jackson told every one to get out of the car. "We're busted guys, you've got' a get out, hide until they go by and try to hike back to Washington" As he slowed the car Fred and Ritchie jumped out the back door and headed into the woods. The new man who was in the passenger seat determined that the police car probably wasn't after us. "I'm taking my chances with you," he said.

Fred and Ritchie had barely touched the ground when Jackson pulled off hoping that the police car would not see the drop-off. They drove off doing well above any speed limit judging by the fact that they were momentarily leaving the police car far behind. Jackson' car began to slow down even though his foot was still buried in the throttle. In a matter of seconds the police car behind turned around and headed the other direction, giving Jackson a reason to breath a sigh of relief.

Though the car Jackson was in was barely moving he wondered if he should go back and pick up Fred and Ritchie since the police car had apparently turned around and joined the others.

"See, I told you they didn't make us. Fred and them are stupid. They walk'n for nut'n." What a bragging idiot Jackson thought as he continued to rattle off his professional views. "We don't got to go back and get'm, they shouldn't-na whimped out," he continued to rattle. At the next intersection Jackson told him he was going back to get the others. Jackson was feeling a little better knowing there was no need for them to walk or hitch-hike all the way back to D.C. He, the passenger, was still rattling off when they came to steep grade on the highway. Now barely moving along, Jackson looked through the rear view mirror and noticed a set of slow moving head lights that had been coming up behind them and coming on tremendously fast. One more glance in the rear view mirror revealed that they had suddenly turned on the flashing red and white lights.

"U'm gon'na pull to the side of the road and we'll jump out and run for it. We'll call the car in stolen." Jackson said "but first we've got to put some space between us and them." Jackson floored the gas pedal.

"Please don't" George begged, "let's just give up." Instead of giving up, Jackson sped up to nearly eighty miles per hour before realizing that his passenger was right. They would probably get hurt or hurt someone by trying to get away. He slowed down as they approached a four police cars blockade awaiting their arrival and the pursuing car now driving right against their rear bumper.

"Get out of the car and put your hands on the hood now!" This was the roaring voice of a Maryland State trooper. They did as they were told. While being handcuffed behind their backs, George began squeal. "I was just hitching a ride, what did he do?" he asked.

"Nothing," said the officer, "we just want to ask you some questions." At the state police barracks he was handcuffed with his rattle mouthed comrade still insisting he should go on his way.

"I don't know that man," he kept saying. Jackson needed to get him out of there or he would surely go down.

"I just picked him up about an hour ago hitchhiking. He's right," Jackson said, "I don't know him at all." They asked for his identification, go it, and told him he was free to go. This was a good sign; the police wouldn't have done that if they were in real deep shit. "What's in your trunk," the policeman asked. As Jackson thought about what he had inside the trunk, he realized there were two walkie-talkies and he remembered that there was a drawn map of the liquor store location. He changed the subject without answering and said, "I'd like to first report a lot of shooting as I passed a building up the highway, it looked like a fight or something," He said while taking the trunk key off the twisted piece of wire and putting it into the palm of his other hand.

"We know about it," he answered. "I don't have the key to trunk. My mother gave me the car today and I was driving it back to D.C. when I stopped for all the police cars. I guess I didn't know just how fast I was going," Jackson said.

Reynolds, he asked, "we've detained your son. No, he's not under arrest; we'd like to know if you gave him the car this morning. No he didn't have an accident. We're just checking to make sure it wasn't stolen. No he hasn't done anything wrong we're just . . . . No, I told you this was just a routine stop. There was a problem in the area and we just wanted to ask a few questions. What time did your son leave with the car that you gave him . . . Okay . . . did he have anyone with him? Listen . . . Mrs. Reynolds . . . Listen. Never mind. I am sorry to take up your time." As he hung up, Jackson knew his mother was about to drive the policeman crazy with questions of her own and would not answer anything.

"Well Mr. Reynolds," he said, I'll tell you this, you guys were lucky tonight. I'm not saying you've done anything, but if you have, this is klu klux klan territory and I'd like to put them all in jail about what happen over at that so called liquor store operation, but I can't. But I advise you boys not to come back here and tangle with them red necks. I have a feeling you know what I'm talking about. So take your asses out of here and pick up your friends, their waling about five miles down on Rte. 40 east. Let us handle the clan, you just stay away from them boys, you hear?" "Yeah," Jackson answered while scurrying toward the exit.

He picked up the new man and then Fred and Ritchie further down the highway. He knew they had been set up to be forced into a fight with the clan, but why? And why not tell them so they could have had a chance? They could have easily been killed, by folks who would have enjoyed the killing and they wouldn't have spent one day in jail.

A few weeks later and a little more prepared. They drove back up Rte 40 west to see just what was behind the liquor store. Apparently it was used as a training ground for the clansmen and the liquor supply store sold ammunitions, weapons and survival materials. They did rip off the supply store on one Sunday afternoon in broad daylight while the Clan was playing military games in the woods.

Chapter 22

Jackson snuck into Pittsburgh and went to his mother's new home in Library Pennsylvania. He had developed the mumps and was suffering from a high temperature and all the misery that comes with the mumps at age twenty-four.

That night, he was awakened by a nightmare that had caused him to cry out in his sleep. Everyone in the house was awakened by his screams that were caused by illusions due to fever and fatigue. He was afraid and told everyone trying to enter the room to stay away from him. He remembered thinking that everyone, including Gloria, was some sort of demon.

While he was alone trembling with chills in his mother entered the bedroom. At first he thought that she too was just another demon and told her to get out. Of course she'd never been afraid of him and as always she said, "no matter how old you get or big you get, I'll always be your mother. I brought you into this world and I would surely take you out of this world if you ever disrespect me."

She sat on the edge of the bed and spoke to him.

"I want you to listen to me" she said. "I love you so much," to that date he couldn't remember his mother ever saying I love you. She then gently squeezed his hand with one hand while feeling his forehead with her other. Without another word she kissed his forehead and said, "son; I'm worried about you. I never want to see you sick. I need you to be the big strong man that you are." Jackson wasn't sure if he was not hallucinating or dreaming that he was hearing such warm words of compassion and additionally being touched and even kissed by Ruth Reynolds. She had always expressed the love she had for him through threats of 'wringing his neck' or 'whipping his little ass' for being so bad.

"I'm sick too" she said. "My heart is broken and now I'm told I may not live another year." Jackson's mother lived all her life known to him loving two men. One that worked as hard as any man could trying to keep his family fed and happy and the other, who was the birth father of Jackson and his four younger brothers and sisters, who was very busy being a man of his own in crowd. Jackson believed she loved both of them with no way to release one without causing her own life to fall apart. Somehow, she had gotten strong enough to leave Charlie Reynolds; who Jackson called daddy and to buy a house to set up a home with his biological father who he called Beb.

After all the years of clinging to Beb and mothering five of his children Beb apparently choose to settle down and get married, but it was to another woman. Jackson's mother, who had finally found the courage to leave the safety and security of home to pursue the love of her life, was left to piece together what had gone wrong and to face a coming death alone.

She told Jackson she had cancer and was dying. "Don't let me down" she said. "You are more like Charles than any of them. I know you'll take care of your brothers and sister. You've got'ta get well now and grow up right this minute. We need you son; I need you"

Jackson was saddened with emotion. Only this time his tears did not fall inside onto his heart like a warrior and the way a man is supposed to cry; this time his tears ran down his face like a boy cries when he's lost and yearns for his momma. She did not shed a tear. She simply watched Jackson weep until he went off to sleep.

Jackson could not stay in the Pittsburgh area long without being arrested. Within a few days he went back to Washington with Gloria, Sandy, his third daughter and Ivy, who had just turn three months old. He was back where he could live hidden amongst the blacks of the Nation's capital.

On December 14, 1970, just three weeks before his mother died. He was going into Pittsburgh to visit her. He felt so bad for her; a woman with seven children, two men and a slew of friends was by some strange fate dying lonely. Her weight was down to sixty pounds. She had broken her arm trying to get off of her hospital bed. She was suffering tremendously. He had to see her once again so that he could say, I love you mom, for the first time in his recollection.

Jackson and his brother Rocky drove into town. The four hour drive had taken them just inside of three hours in his hopped up Roadrunner automobile. Just as they exited the Pennsylvania Turnpike, the car unexplainably shut down. After an hour of trying to determine why this one year old vehicle refused to start he turned the key and it started.

They drove into Oakland where the hospital was located on 5th Avenue. Just as they turned onto Forbes Avenue which was a block away, the engine mysteriously shut down again, again no logical reason. The time was nearly five thirty; visiting hours were going to be over soon. He could not chance spending the night in Pittsburgh. After a few frustrating moments he again turned the key and she started as if nothing was wrong. They had just turned onto Fifth Avenue, one block from the hospital driveway when for the third time the engine just stopped dead. Before he could get out of the car he looked up into the facing traffic to see three police cars, one from Beaver County, one of the Pittsburgh Police Department and the other, an Allegheny County unmarked car were all filled with detectives. They were all waiting for his visit so they could serve whatever warrants that were outstanding. Apparently, the bed of his dying mother was an excellent place to make a long awaited arrest. Ironically, one of the waiting officers was his first cousin and he had probably set up the whole trap.

Just as Jackson looked up into the eyes of the policemen they look right back and into his. The chase was about to start. Instantly Jackson's Roadrunner started and he was behind the wheel in a flash. He made an immediate right turn onto the street the police were on and put his petal to the floor. In his rear view mirror he could see that the first car had stalled in the middle of the intersections and that the second car had rear ended the first. They were all just getting out of their vehicles. He could only guess, not really knowing what was going on.

As he rounded the next corner, he got out of the car and instructed Rocky to drive away, thinking they would call ahead and have the car stopped and arrest him. As Rocky drove off he walked towards the street where the police were still trying to start the first car. The second car was still steaming from hitting the first. The third car was gone and he assume out on the chase.

Jackson went to the hospital lobby and called someone to come and get him. Then he called his mother's room. "Son," she said in a very weak and unfamiliar voice. "Don't come here, the police have been around here all day waiting to arrest you. I prayed you wouldn't be caught." Somehow, he knew her prayers were answered. He wanted to see her once more, just to say good-bye. Of course he couldn't stay away. If it meant that he would go to jail, then so be it, he just simply had to see her. He put on his most ferocious look and boldly went to her room without hesitation and without care or fear. He sat by her bed side for more than an hour without saying anything. Her eyes were closed but she didn't seem to be sleeping. With each breath that she took came a frightening sound as if it may be her last. She was doing so poorly that Jackson actually found himself praying that she could pass away and avoid any more of the pain that she was going through. He wished that she could some how in her final moments, not have to worry about him but more importantly that she didn't have to worry about her two teenage children that she would have to leave behind. He wished that he could make it so she needn't worry about any of the many things that her mind must take her through upon her death bed. And yet there he sat as helpless as man could get. He couldn't take seeing her like that any longer. Without a word he stood up to leave as she reached out and grabbed his hand.

"Wait son," she whispered. "Sit down for another moment I want to say something to you." She paused for a long while as if thinking of what she wanted to say. Jackson sat nervously, at times fearfully thinking that she had stopped breathing while he waited for her to continue her words. She finally opened her eyes again and gestured for him to lean closer. She said; "son I know I was sometimes a little hard on you as a boy. It wasn't that I didn't love you, it was because I didn't know how else to teach you when you seem to know so much." She paused again for a few minutes and continued as if she was talking to me as a small boy. She said, "I know you didn't burn down the church but I wanted you to tell me how you new the church was going to burn down." Jackson didn't know what she was talking about, but as she paused once more he vividly recalled as a little boy at five years old he had told her that he had dreamed that Jesus' church on their street was going to burn down just so that His Daddy (His, meaning Jesus) could fix it up. He remembered that on one very rare occasion as a child his mother made him go to church with one of the neighbors. While at church he couldn't take his eyes off of the dilapidated condition that God's house was in. And when they began to speak of Jesus, and say that it was Jesus' house and not God's, who was Jesus' father, he assumed that just like his dad was fixing up their home; God would come and fix up the house of Jesus. That Sunday night he had a horrific nightmare that the devil had burned down God's house. The next morning his mother asked him what he had dreamed last night because she believed that she had often hit the numbers when he told her of his dreams. He now remembered telling her that 'God's house had burned to the ground'. A few days later in the middle of the night the light from the blazing church down the street awakened him. He watched for a long while as the flames engulfed the entire building before waking his mother to tell her that his dream had come true and that this time it was no dream. The next morning she told Jackson not to tell anyone about his dream for fear that someone would think he was evil. Jackson, until now, had forgotten all about the incident and had put it completely out of his memory.

She went on to say, "Since that day I wasn't sure if you were blessed or cursed. The one thing that I did know is that I wanted you to be just a normal boy. You've turned out to be a strong hearted man and I really don't know where you got it from. Now I need you to help me. I want you to get out of here. I don't want you to see me this way because I know how you and your brothers and sisters are. You get away and get away now before they get you. God will show you the way." Jackson didn't know what to make of his mother's statement; but after saying that, she closed her eyes and he sat there for a while before realizing that she wasn't going to speak again.

When he turned to go he said, "Ma, I love ya; your gon'na be okay, you just watch. I know your gon'na be okay."

"I love you to boy"

Ruth Reynolds died January 5, 1971 at the age of forty-nine. 'Well at least she lived to be forty-nine.' Jackson thought at the time that that was an old age. Of course, the police were at the funeral hoping he would show up. Needless to say, they were disappointed. He stood idle by as they buried his mother. She left behind two men of love, four sons, three daughters, many friends and yet a year after her death her grave site had never been visited by anyone other than himself. His guess was that, when a person expresses his or her love spiritually, the only love in return is spiritual and without a desire to acknowledge that she has really gone. To some it may seem disrespectful, but Jackson understood. As he matured, he personally found the need to visit her grave; just because of the vanity of thinking she may be somewhere emotionally hurt and feeling that no one cares. And just in case that may be true, he tells her "I'm here and we all love you. We just know you know it, without the customary showing of respect for the place where your body lies."

All of his life he has been convinced that there were guardian angels that watch over each and every individual. And that God, after doing all of His marvelous creating gave a command that, His human creations, their seeds and all the seeds of their children and their children's children, forever be assigned Gods own angels to watch over and to interfere as an act in response to a sacrificial prayer by the guardians and only the guardian. Jackson believed that at a time when her prayers should have been for herself, she felt the need to pray for someone else's well-being; that person being him. It may sound silly to most, but the mysterious way his car shut down causing him to elude a trap and the final shut down and start up just as the police car shut down seemed nothing short of a miracle. If he had been arrested he would have been taken from his family and sentenced to five to ten years in prison, as promised by a Beaver County judge. The thought of what may have become of his children and those that he loves, with him away in prison frightened him to this very day.

Learning of his guardian angel he was convinced that she exists and always had caused him to adjust his focus at the right time. By doing so, he committed himself to being the guardian that would willingly kill or die to try and protect those harmlessly exposed to the wrath of the greedy that rob folks of their dignity.

As his mother requested, he needed to grow up quickly and become able to constructively position himself. First to help himself and then onto all that he could do for his own. This became his personal task. He could easily admit that he failed in many aspects of life, but in his own mind he would, no matter what, succeed in his attempt to become a sword of God.

Chapter 23

The death of Martin Luther King did make a bit of a difference in most of the inner cities across the county. For those few days of rioting they were recognized as a people who had taken all they could take. And they had finally sent a message, though a weak one, that, 'they just may be brave enough to retaliate if pushed to far'.

The movement began to come to a halt as meaningful jobs became more available. Access to college and a better education with educational grants and student loans were being made available immediately. More young blacks were given confidence in the fact that a change was brewing.

During all the pacifying activities Jackson and a friend decided to open a dry cleaning business. Ironically, it was just across the Maryland State line at Wheeler Road and Southern Avenue, exactly where they had confronted the National Guard on April 6, 1998; just four years earlier.

This wasn't his first venture into business. During the movement activities they had attempted the dry cleaning business before; in addition to his ongoing effort in the construction business. His true desire was always in the construction arena. Like his dad, he wanted to build. He was in love with prideful feeling of making a building grow right up out of the ground by the strength of his own hands. From 1969 through 1972 and onward he was always building room additions, kitchens and bathrooms to subsidize his income.

The dry cleaning business venture was in addition to his construction business. They named their dry cleaner, The House of Clayton; after his best friend's sir name.

The dry cleaners had been an existing and fully equipped previously owned business. It had been abandoned by its owners after the riots. The actually dollar value of the equipment was about fifty thousand dollars and way out of their reach.

They had their eyes out looking for a place to start a dry cleaner business for quite some time. When they were informed that this dry cleaners was completely equipped and hadn't been damaged by the riots, Jackson approached the owner of the small shopping center and asked if he would be interested in renting the store front which was a boarded up section in a strip mall with a liquor store currently open and doing a lucrative business. He gave no indication that he was interested in the cleaning equipment; in fact, he volunteered to remove and dispose of it for the building owners in exchange for three months free rent. The strip mall owner agreed to his terms and signed a two year lease for the space to use as they saw fit.

After the lease was secured, they opened the business, with the fifty thousand dollars worth of equipment and a loan using the equipment as collateral. The equipment and the business now belonged to Jackson and the owners were unable to change the leasing terms. All total, they were in ownership of a new dry cleaning plant; fully and modernly equipped, including counters and unclaimed clothes on motor driven tracks, all for a three hundred dollar rent deposit and the start up cost of hangers and cleaning fluid. This was the biggest opportunity of Jackson's life and certainly a deal of a life time. All they needed was customers.

Within ninety days the cleaners was grossing close to five thousand dollars a week at the store. They brought in Freddie Morris who started a pick-up and delivery service with three new trucks, black owner and operated. They advertised as "the best cleaners in town". They started negotiating with the black drivers from one of the largest dry cleaners in Washington, D. C. Most of their drivers began lining up customers for The House of Clayton, recommending theirs over their own employer.

Within a year their gross reached eight thousand dollars per week and growing. In the second year of business they bided and landed a cleaning contract from the United State Marine Core Marching Band which meant over eight hundred uniforms monthly. They were in a legitimate business, big time. All made possible by that one three hundred dollar investment.

In two years they had grossed nearly one million dollars. They had seventeen employees and three delivery drivers. Life had made a turn for the best. Jackson worked from 6:00 a.m. until 10:00 p.m. seven days a week. No time for protest, no time for rallies. He now hungered for success. He was in the American mainstream, a proud nigga wheel'n and deal'n like George Jefferson. No need to plot a crime. They hired their comrades who were more trustworthy than anyone could ever imagine. The system they had fought so hard to disrupt was now swallowing them up in acceptance. This is how America works, they say. This is what freedom is about, they say. Being successful brought the pride that he was always unknowingly in search of.

By 1974, he had five daughters; the last two being Ivy and Jackie. He began to forget the struggle. Some of his friends stayed with it, but as time past by the Black Power Movement in D. C. was like handfuls of sand. The harder they grasp the quicker it disappeared. Racism again changed its appearance and took on a form that was much harder to recognize.

Business eventually became a 'the usual'. The pace had slowed for Jackson. One after another the inner circle began to dissolve. They all began to grow up. Some took the drug route and ultimately self destructed. Others settled in to jobs and the raising of children. A lot of the 409 ended up serving time for one crime or another.

Jackson remained wanted by the system and never able to get at ease in the presence of unmarked cars or flashing lights in his rear view mirror.

With the money he earned, he brought a new house in the Oxon Hill area just south of Washington, D. C. And then came additional cars, the purchase of a night club, called the Southeast Underground which was directly across the street from where Jimmy Warren had been shot and killed seven years earlier. He expanded his construction company and focused on contracts in the fifty thousand dollar range.

Audrey and Sherry lived with him every opportunity he got to bring them home. They were fortunate to have two mothers who loved them. They were never shortened of affection by their sisters. When they were with Jackson, they didn't want to go back to Joyce. When they were with their mother it was always difficult to taken them away. They always wanted to come, but were sadden at times to be unable to bring the other vital parts of their lives along.

The Odes of Jackson

On this day I Commit my life as a warrior for the God of love of which a piece of him lies in the hearts of all those who wish to harm no one. Those that live only to survive and dwell in peace. Those that pursue all of the compassion they can gain from their fellow man. I am one that desires a Christ-like passion rather than the vengeance of a god.

I want to love and be loved. I want to wipe away the tears of others. I want to lend my shoulder to those that need to cry. I want to stand back to back with one that would fight and die for those that need protected from evil. "Chose me God," I say there would be no greater death than to die fighting at the side of a warrior who battles at the feet of the All Mighty.

On this night I feel the fears that men feel on their most lonely and darkened night. I feel locked in a cell. I feel fear of being chased by a predator until cornered and made to kneel in preparation of dying . . . or to stand and fight for my life and the lives of the helpless.

On this day my eyes are opened, no devil to fear. There is no such thing as demons or evil spirits. No where to place my blame. There are only dark rooms where I cannot see how harmless an empty space can be. There is only a mountain and I don't know what lies on the other side. There is only a valley that I can't see how deep the bottom lies. There is only a unknown face of a man that I don't know how to love; a white face, a yellow face, a colorless face . . . There is no one and nothing to fear but there are many good warriors to embrace."

Chapter 24

Jackson was what you might call settling down. At age 30, he had become a normal hardworking man. No drugs, he had never touched them. Liquor, he had never found the desire to make himself look like a fool and vowed not to ever get drunk. To him it stood to reason that a man cannot be a man if he's staggering around or falling from the effects of liquor or other mind altering drugs that take away your ability to protect yourself and family.

In 1979, fourteen years after going to Washington, D. C. he began to yearn for home. He missed what he remembered as simplicity. He wanted his daughters to enjoy the safety of Coverdale, Pa., to be able to safely play in the street in front of the house he was raised in. To enjoy the benefits of knowing your neighbors by name and sharing memories of when you were kids and having the same neighbors for more than fifty years.

He realized that being born and raised in a small coal mining town was the blessing of his lifetime. Sometimes a man can look high and low and in every direction for his true place in life. Some get stupid and stumble off into a life of self inflicted misery, some look to God, some look to out distant their peers by ways of education and financial success. They race off to nowhere and find themselves naked and without roots. But in some rare instances happiness can be found in places you've passed by; in people you once knew. In his case, it was in a place where he didn't have to be better than his neighbors, just respected and unharmed by them.

Charles Reynolds, Jackson dad, gave him the house that he was born in. He worked, with his father's help, to enlarge it to his family's size. His kids adjusted quickly to the little town joys. On September 3, 1980 there was a knock on his front door. The phone was ringing off the hook. When he answered, it was Carrie who lived across the street hysterically telling him that the police were out in front of the house.

His instinct, after so many years of running and avoiding the law was to hide or find away out the back. He looked through the rear curtains, there were two police cars out back; they had encircled his father's house. He knew it was over. His five girls were asking what was going on. They were frighten and in tears.

He went to the front door where a group of policemen were waiting to arrest him.

"Jackie Reynolds" the police officer said. "I haven't seen you in fifteen years." "Listen Jackie we're going to have to place you under arrest for flight to avoid prosecution and a bench warrant issued by a Beaver County judge for burglary and receiving stolen goods." He continued on to say "I wish you had taken care of this long ago. I don't believe I've ever served a fourteen year old warrant. I'm really sorry." By now Jackson's neighbors had come out onto the street wanting to know why he was being bothered after all those years. One of the small home town policemen responded by saying, they had no choice.

As he stuck his hand forward to be cuffed his youngest daughter Jackie ran to him and started to fight and cry as he was being taken from the house. He paused and said "I'll be all right." Gloria and all five girls were in tears. He wondered if coming home was the right choice. The folks in his community were outraged but held their peace. As he was driven off the girls had come out onto the front yard and were waving good-bye.

He was driven to the Beaver County jail where upon his arrival the judge that had waited so long to inflict his wrath of justice made a special trip to be there and to welcome him back. "Nearly fifteen years" he said. "I knew I would get you back eventually, everyone else gave up on you. I promised you five years hard time and now I get the last laugh."

If Jackson could have, he would have killed him where he stood. He took Jackson from all that was dear to him. As if it was a game. The judge smiled and said "It's my turn now."

Folks from Coverdale to Washington, D.C. came and tried everything possible to get him released, to no avail.

It had been seventeen years since he had sat in confinement. Days, weeks and then months went by. The judge had refused to talk to anyone about his case.

Hope had dwindled; the possibility that he would be finally sentenced to five to ten years was becoming a reality.

Finally after hundreds of letters from friends and sympathizing politicians the judge set a sentencing date. It was two days before

Thanksgiving. The courtroom was filled with people who had come from Washington, D.C. and Maryland. Of course, most of Coverdale was there in support of this, now small business man with five daughters. After six or seven character witness, reading of pleading letters for Jackson's release the judge looked over his glasses and demanded that he approach the bench for sentence.

"In all my thirty years on the bench I have never received so many letters and phone calls on behalf of a prisoner" he said. "However justice must be served. After careful consideration, I sentence you; Jackson Thomas Reynolds to five years of hard time." After a long pause and a quite disappointed courtroom. He continued "Ninety-days served and four years and six months probation. If you have managed to not be arrested this long, four years should be no problem."

Everyone in the court room seemed to sigh at the same time. It meant that he was going home today. It was over. Fourteen years of hiding and running from the law to avoid arrest was finally over. After ninety days in the Beaver County jail he was heading home to his life with to watch his children grow and await the time to tell them about his life as a kid.

Of the ten key members of the 409 only five lived past the age of twenty five. None of the following heroes survived the riot's aftermath.

* **Eddie Brooks** was killed by the Atlanta police while in custody for a traffic violation. According to those who viewed his body he appeared to have been badly beaten. The coroner declared that he died of intestinal blockage.
* **Ronald Allen** (El-Tez) was shot in the back supposedly by a woman's disgruntled boyfriend. No body was recovered; he was never seen again.
* **Jimmie Bolden** was shot to death during the Martin Luther King riots by national guardsmen
* **Bobby Lusha** was arrested in Philadelphia in summer of 1968, supposedly by the F.B.I., he was never seen again.
* **Smittie Richardson** was found dead while sitting at a traffic light in Washington D. C. According to a family member that identified his body, he appeared to have been badly beaten. The coroner stated that he had died of a brain aneurysm.

Jackson reached the golden age of thirty at which time this story ends. Most people believe that life truly begins at thirty; Jackson was not most people. His life began at birth and never ended. As this story winds to its end; any reader can see that for some unexplained reason Jackson truly had a story to tell. He had all of the early markings of a young man that wouldn't live long, at least, not as a free man. Yet he reached the age of thirty without a criminal record. He reached the age of thirty and beyond without any use of drugs or alcohol. Without ever smoking a cigarette. He reached the age of thirty without ever attending church or anything similar to a church. He made it without any known enemies other than those that may hate black men for being black.

By the year 1975, most of the 409 had met their life's end at the hands of policemen and others fell to street violence or other obstacles that prevent the success of merely reaching an average life span. Of course those that died at the hands of our neighborhood police officers became victims of the infamous 'justifiable homicides.' And, those that died at the hands of our brothers became the victims a new form of genocide. There are those who managed to kill for the thrill of Cain, but they were always considered crazy and released back onto the block.

No matter how many homicides occur, other than war time deaths, blacks that die by the sword statistically out number any of the other races by far. Jackson had been shot at five times on five different occasions before his twentieth birthday. Four times by police officers and once by another black youth.

He is eligible to give testimony that, if you indulge in a life of crime no matter what the cause, there is a good chance that you will die by the sword. He can testify that whether you commit a crime or not, if you're a young black male who comes out at night any where in America there is a good chance that you may end up imprisoned or dead. An understatement in America is that being a black man has it's disadvantages; so does being poor, blind, cripple, or crazy. It seems that being identified as different brings out the worst in a human. As men we have been instilled with greed, selfishness, jealousy, envy, the negative list could go on and on. The only way to separate oneself from life's negative grip is to stay sober and true to your passions of doing the right thing. Stand quickly to defend the rights of those that are less fortunate. Focus on your own ability to live in harmony. Work hard to understand the makeup of the rules of common sense in lieu of commandments. Attempt to change your rules that are not in rhythm with the well-being of all of mankind. Know that rules are placed as an effort to provide a way to live in harmony. Rules are likened to the creation of a well orchestrated choir. Many voices can be added and the harmony of the choir continues to be enhanced in volume and glory, however, this heavenly sound can be crippled by one wayward voice. Like a song out of time or a key out of tune, the pleasant sound of harmony can turn to noise. When our voices become accustom to noise we all begin to play a part in life's music without synchronization. We forget the rules that are needed to create the sweetness of togetherness. We lose our rhythm and we fall out of step without harmony and, without God.

Jackson spent a lot of time out of step. He had gotten out of tune and had fallen into the deceptive notion that everything needed to change in order to accommodate the rhythm that he 'thought' was real. Jackson was not alone with his assumptions. The greatest of men, the most famous and even those chosen by God Himself fell from the rules and attempted to dance to their own life's music just to find that selfishness is just another form of foolishness. Yet when all is said and done we forge ahead with hope that somehow the much sought after, sweetness of human harmony, will soon be with us. He learned that, we won't see God until we approach Him with one voice. We need to know the rules of harmony and when we learn, with His help, we will have finally gotten it right.

END OF STORY